W9-CZJ-887

Helping the Bereaved
Celebrate the Holidays

A Sourcebook for Planning
Educational and Remembrance Events

James E. Miller

Willowgreen Publishing

To Jennifer, a jewel,
and to Clare, a gem.

I am indebted to several people with whom I worked to plan and bring
into being a community-wide holiday event for bereaved people several
years ago. I learned much from them: Chaplain Joe Andrews, Delores
Bastian, Sr. Jeana Bodart, Phyllis Hermann, Patrice Masbaum, Debra
Noell, Dar Richardson, and Rabbi Richard Safran. I am especially indebted
to Jennifer Levine for all she did for those early events and for all she has
done since those days to support me in my creative endeavors. She shares
her knowledge unselfishly and she offers her feedback unguardedly. This
is her book too.

Copyright © 1997 James E. Miller

All rights reserved.

Willowgreen Publishing
PO Box 25180
Fort Wayne, Indiana 46825
219/424-7916

Library of Congress Catalogue
Card Number: 97-90913

ISBN 1-885933-25-8

Preface

Five years ago the first edition of *Helping the Bereaved Celebrate the Holidays* appeared. It grew out of the experiences of a group of concerned professionals who created an annual preparing-for-the-holidays event for bereaved people in Fort Wayne, Indiana. Its purpose was to share some basic ideas with others who had not yet tried such a program.

The demand for this writing was greater than expected. It appears people in various settings, including hospitals, hospices, congregations, funeral homes, and community organizations, are recognizing the importance of providing support to those who are grieving during a difficult time of the year.

Much has changed in five years. There's more knowledge about loss and grief in general. There's greater acceptance of the value of rituals. There's more openness for public discussion of issues relating to death and mourning. Grief support groups have sprouted up in many locations, along with the creation of help-for-the-holidays events all across North America. It seemed appropriate, therefore, to create this revised and expanded edition. I hope it proves useful.

Jim Miller
September 1, 1997

Other Works by James E. Miller

Books

When You Know You're Dying
One You Love Is Dying
When You're Ill or Incapacitated / When You're the Caregiver
What Will Help Me? / How Can I Help?
How Will I Get Through the Holidays?
Winter Grief, Summer Grace
Autumn Wisdom
The Caregiver's Book
Welcoming Change
A Pilgrimage Through Grief
A Little Book for Preachers

Audiotapes

The Transforming Potential of Your Grief
When You're Ill or Incapacitated

Videotapes

Invincible Summer
Listen to Your Sadness
How Do I Go On?
Nothing Is Permanent Except Change
Why Yellow?
Common Bushes Afire
By the Waters of Babylon
We Will Remember
Gaining a Heart of Wisdom
Awaken to Hope
Be at Peace
The Natural Way of Prayer
You Shall Not Be Overcome
The Grit and Grace of Being a Caregiver

Introduction

Let's begin by being clear about what this book is not. It's not a book about how to get through the holidays when you're grieving the death of someone you've loved. Nor is it a book about how professionals can apply certain healing skills in working with those who are grieving during a critical time of the year. Those books have already been written.

This book has a single focus: how to plan, design, and carry out an event or a series of events to help grieving individuals face the holidays in healthy, healing ways. These events carry different titles, such as "help for the holidays," "grief and the holidays," "how to make the most of the holidays," and various other names. The title isn't as important as what happens at these events. Useful information about the grief process is offered. Ideas for making it through the approaching holidays are shared. Opportunities are provided for people to talk and listen to one another, to tell stories and compare notes, to laugh and to cry. Usually there's a way to commemorate the lives of those who have died. Often there's an effort to provide back-up resources or follow-up care.

These events can be planned by different sorts of groups. Hospices often sponsor them, offering care for the survivors of those who have died while at the same time increasing the visibility of the work of hospice. Congregations sometimes sponsor them, either for their own members or for the larger community. It's not unusual for clusters of congregations to work together. Hospitals have also shown an interest, as have community counseling centers and certain self-help groups. In some situations funeral homes are taking the lead. In others it's a cemetery association that commits its resources. In a few cases a single individual or family provides most of the drive.

Increasingly we're finding that coalitions of organizations and individuals can be especially effective in implementing these plans. The base of support is broader. The areas of expertise are greater. Often there's a synergy when people from different fields work together for the good of someone else. The topic, of course, is serious, but the experience of planning and executing these events can be invigorating and fun. It can even lead in unexpected and exciting directions.

One thing that often happens with these help-for-the-holidays events is that, when the day rolls around, the response is greater than expected. When they're well publicized and presented in inviting ways, these programs can bring out standing-room-only crowds. They tend to touch a responsive chord in people who are seriously searching for help at a difficult period in their lives. These events meet a need that is not being met in any other way. They promise hope at a time when hope is in short supply. They foster a sense of companionship when loneliness strikes deeply.

Once a program like this has been initiated, it's much easier to repeat it in the future. Sometimes a program like this seems to take on a life of its own, as ideas are expanded and new people come forward to offer their services. It's not uncommon for those who are bereaved to attend two or more years in a row. Nor is it uncommon for those who have been participants in the past to want to serve as planners and facilitators two or three years later. These experiences can also lead to offshoots: support groups, social activities, training programs, special events for other times of the year.

If there's one thing to keep in mind as you consider an event for your community, it's this: you will do best if you make this experience distinctively your own. What works well for one location may not work as well for another. The people you attract may not have the same needs as the people another group attracts. And the people who plan and lead your experience will have their own unique kinds of expertise to be called forth and built upon. Give yourself the freedom and the flexibility to do what seems best, given who you are and whom you want to serve, realizing that you'll learn equally from your mistakes and from your successes. May your mistakes be less than serious and more than profitable. And may your successes exceed your dreams.

1

Understanding the Situation

Before looking into the specifics of planning a program for the bereaved as the holidays draw near, it will help to be clear about the situation these folks face. Usually it's a time of persistent stress. Or more accurately, it's a period of *multiple* stresses, including three major ones.

The Stress of Holiday Time

The holidays are a time charged with emotion.

For some people, these are wonderful times. Their moods are especially cheerful. They look forward to the preparations and festivities with genuine eagerness and joy.

For many, however, and perhaps for most, the holidays are a mixed blessing. The season's traditions and celebrations are fun to plan for and to carry out...and at the same time, they're *not* so fun. The pace can grow hectic. The pressures can become demanding. The cultural expectations of what makes for true holiday happiness may leave one feeling disappointed, disillusioned, and somehow empty. There's even an expression for this experience: "the holiday blues." Many of us carry an idealized image of what the holidays should be like and how we should feel all along the way. Ideals, as everyone knows, are difficult to live up to.

Then there are those for whom the holidays are approached with wariness or fear or even dread. Some people carry scars from previous holiday experiences. Sometimes finances can be a worry or a threat. Family members may clash with one another, or they may avoid one another. Either way, it can mar what is supposed to be a special time. Sometimes abuse may go unchecked. Deep hurts may go unacknowledged. Guilt may go unresolved.

In short, holidays may turn out to be less than picture perfect. Sometimes it's a slight gnawing feeling one has. Other times it's like a stabbing pain. However it's felt, the urge is the same: to put the holidays behind oneself as soon as convenient, if not as soon as possible. And that produces another kind of stress.

The Stress of Grief

The experience of grief is more than the inward response to another's death. It presents its own tensions which must be looked at and dealt with if they're to be overcome and resolved.

A time of grief is a strange time. Familiar patterns of life are changed, either temporarily or permanently. Everyday routines are disrupted, creating uneasiness and even pain. What you used to take for granted, you no longer can. The one you love is gone and their absence is palpable. But it's more than just this one loss that's involved. Depending upon who has died and the surrounding family circumstances, you may have to move to another home, or take another job, or endure financial hardship, or lose the companionship of those who have supported you in the past.

Psychological stressors are commonplace. People in grief often experience anxiety and fear on top of their sadness and loneliness. They may surprise themselves with the anger they feel, with or without good reason. Chances are they'll experience a loss of self-esteem—most grievers do. They'll probably invest precious energy being preoccupied with the one who is gone. They're likely to struggle with helplessness—the helplessness of being unable to change what has happened and the helplessness of being unable to control their roller coaster feelings.

The physical reactions that accompany grief can also add to their stress. People commonly report a tightness in their throat and chest, a real pain in the area of their heart, or an irregular heartbeat. Other symptoms may include nausea, diarrhea, dizziness, trembling, hot flashes, headaches. These are all normal responses to grief.

Behavioral changes can also create tension for the one who is grieving. That person is likely to feel tired a great deal of time, and perhaps as never before. They may suffer serious sleep disturbances, unusual dreams, even nightmares. They may lose all appetite, or eat more than they ever have. Something similar may happen with their sexual behavior. They may cling to others uncharacteristically. On top of all this, and because of all this, they may wonder if they're going crazy—that's a natural reaction.

Spiritual stressors can also occur. Someone who's grieving may find it harder to practice their traditional religious observances. One's relationship with God may undergo serious challenge and change. They may struggle to find meaning in the face of all that has happened.

Not all grievers will feel all these stresses. But every griever will feel stress of one sort or another, unless they block it from their mind and attempt to feel nothing at all. And then that's a stress all its own that will eventually have to be dealt with.

The Stress Caused by Others

It used to be that death was more accepted as a part of daily life. People were more familiar with death because they lived closer to the earth, closer to the rhythms of nature, closer to animals. Children died more frequently than they do today. Adults died at younger ages. And when death occurred, family and friends were active participants in all that happened afterward—the preparation of the body, the wake, the funeral service, the burial.

It also used to be that mourning was more a part of everyday life. People dressed in black to show what they were feeling inside and so others would be aware of what had happened in their life. Men wore arm bands and women wore veils. Mourning wreaths were attached to front doors. The bereaved were expected to do certain things and avoid doing other things for prescribed periods of time, and everyone knew what those things were.

Today we treat death and grief differently in most North American cultures. We're not as comfortable dealing with it. Many of us avoid talking about death by using various euphemisms: we say "he went sleep" or "she went to her peace" rather than "he died" or "she is dead." Or we may avoid the topic by not using any words at all—we may ignore the subject and refuse to converse with the bereaved about what's happening to them. We may expect people to get through their grief as quickly as possible, and if it's not fast enough, we may try to hurry them along. We may encourage them to count their blessings, or to put on a happy face, or to be stronger.

Not surprisingly, all these ways of responding to death and grief add to the stress level of those who are bereaved. Their painful feelings are not readily accepted. Their need to talk about their loss, sometimes repeatedly, is not supported. Their natural inclination to allow their grief to take whatever time it takes is not understood. They are made to feel more isolated and alone.

The Rise of "Guerrilla Grief"

The Spanish word *guerrilla* means "small war." Guerrilla warfare is fought by small bands of people, moving quickly and quietly, often under cover of night, staging raids that are meant to surprise the enemy.

There's a sense in which many people today have been subtly encouraged to become "guerrilla grievers." So they let their grief out quickly, so it's not easily seen. They do it quietly, so they're not easily heard. They release their feelings out under cover of night so they won't bother anyone. They keep to themselves. They do what they know they *must* do if they are to heal, but they do it on the sly because they've learned it can be dangerous to do it any other way.

Help-for-the-holidays events attempt to break that cycle. These events communicate, "Your grief is worth talking about." They affirm, "Your story is worth being told." They assure, "Others have taken this journey before you and they have left some lessons for you." Programs like these validate the feelings that grieving people have, give them the opportunity to understand some of what is happening inside, and offer them suggestions for how to make the most of the time before them.

Today grieving people deserve our attention, our respect, and our care. Sponsoring "holiday help" programs is a small but important way to help make that a reality.

2

Defining the Possibilities

Perhaps you've heard about a holiday program that a funeral home in another city has sponsored for several years, attracting more people each time it's offered. You may think to yourself, "All we have to do is copy what they've done and we'll have similar success."

Don't count on it.

Perhaps you've learned about a hospice that has sponsored an annual event, changing it somewhat each year so what they did last year was quite different than what they did five years ago. You may think, "We'll learn from their mistakes and focus only on what they did most recently."

Such an approach may limit how successfully your own event develops.

Perhaps you've read about a congregation that has received rave reviews for a program it puts on just before the holidays each year exclusively for its members. You may presume, "If it works for their people, it will surely work for ours."

Maybe so, maybe not.

Just because an idea works well in one place doesn't mean it will work equally well in all places. Just because one group decides to change their program based on their experiences doesn't mean another program should make similar changes. And just because one group has attracted and pleased one kind of audience doesn't mean you'll attract the same kind of audience or that you'll please in the same way whatever audience you bring out.

Anytime you start anything new, you're traveling in unknown territory. In the case of a new "holiday help" program, you cannot be sure who will come and who will stay away. You cannot know in advance which parts of the program will hit their mark and which will leave something to be desired. You cannot be sure what has really helped someone until you can see it for yourself, and even then you may not know for certain, or you may not realize it until some time afterward.

Tempting as it may be to copy what another group has already done, I suggest you try a different approach. Start not with those other people and what they have done but with yourselves and what you might do. Begin not with their situation but with your own. Familiarize yourself with what others have accomplished, but don't be bound to it. Recognize and respect the uniqueness of your own circumstances and go from there. That's the way you'll meet the most needs and do the most good. And isn't that was really matters?

Start with Questions, Not Answers

There is a series of questions you will do well to ask as you think about developing a "help for the holidays" program.

Why?
Why sponsor a program like this? Is one needed? What makes you think so?

You may be tempted to respond, "Of course this is needed! Look at all those other programs that have sprung up all over the country. Look at the good a program like this can do." That may be true. But just because something *can* be done doesn't mean it *should* be done.

First do your research. Have similar programs been tried in your area before? What happened to them? How long did they last? Are any similar programs already in place? How successful are they? Will you be duplicating efforts? Is such duplication justified? Might you hurt a program that is already working effectively? Is your best solution to start something new or to add your support to something which already exists?

Another kind of research you can do is with those who are in the know. Speak with professionals who deal directly with the bereaved: hospice personnel, clergy, chaplains, social workers, funeral directors, counselors. In their opinion, would a program like this help those for whom it is designed? Would it further the work these professionals already do? Have they heard of similar programs elsewhere? What have they heard about them?

Do your research with the *real* people who are in the know: the bereaved themselves. Do they see the value of something like this? What might be the benefits? Would they attend such an event? Why or why not? Talk with those who aren't grieving at the moment but who can remember what the experience was like for them. What do they think? What does their more distant perspective add?

A related "why" question is this: Why do *you* want to start a program like this? Why is your organization or business interested? What are your motivations? Do you have a burning desire to help the grieving? Why is the desire so burning? Is there any other reason you're doing what you're doing, even if it's only a tiny one? Will this increase your organization's visibility? Will it create good will for your group? Depending upon what your group does, will this be a way to proselytize, to advertise, or to produce income? What are the side benefits for you personally? These questions can be difficult to ask and even more difficult to answer.

Probably there are fewer completely altruistic actions in the world than we would like to think. Even if it's as simple as wanting one's organization to be viewed as caring and concerned, or personally desiring to use one's creativity in the service of others, still there's often a subtle payoff involved.

It goes without saying (and yet we say it here just to be

sure) that the needs of the bereaved should always be at the center of whatever you do. Anything that gets in the way of those needs or displaces those needs is unfair. Anything that takes advantage of the bereaved is unethical.

So ask yourself, "Why do I personally want to do this? Why do we as a group want to do this?" Ask this as you begin. Keep asking it as you continue this work. Be honest so you can keep your work honest.

Who?

There are four important "who" questions you'll need to address at one time or another.

For whom is this event planned?

Is it for those who are grieving the death of a loved one or for those who know other kinds of grief as well? Is it for the recently bereaved or for all bereaved? Is it for the members of a certain group or organization or for the community at large? Is it for adults or children or both? Must you be bereaved to attend? Might friends or parents or colleagues come along? Will professionals be encouraged to attend? You can define your audience in different ways and that will unquestionably impact your program.

Who will plan this event?

Will it be one person or more than one? Will it be an existing group or will a group be formed for just this purpose? Will there be one agency or organization represented, or two, or many? How will these planners be selected? Will they be professionals, or lay, or both?

Who will sponsor this event?

Will it be single or joint sponsorship? What will sponsorship mean? Lending one's name and credibility? Using one's facilities? Providing financial support? Providing in-kind services?

Who will provide leadership at the event itself?

Will there be one speaker or several speakers? A panel of speakers? Workshop leaders? Will these people be trained

16

professionals or will their life experiences qualify them to lead? Will they be chosen from within your group or community, or will they be brought in from somewhere else?

It's easy to see how a lot of people can be involved in an event of this sort, more than you might initially think.

What?
What will be the nature of your event? What will be included in your schedule? What will be excluded? Will it be primarily informational, or inspirational, or both? Will it be a shorter event, say an hour or two? Or will it last longer—a half-day, a full day, or even all weekend?

When?
When will your event take place? Morning, afternoon, or evening? Weekend or weekday? Before the holidays or during them? Once or more than once?

Where?
Will your site be large or small? Will it be your own site or someone else's? Or will it be held at a public location, like an auditorium or a hotel? Or perhaps a school or congregational setting? Or will it be held someplace more private? Will it be held in one area or in adjacent areas, perhaps simultaneously? Will there be more than one site?

Open to your possibilities by opening to questions like these. Don't be in a rush to supply your answers. They will come in time. Trust the process of group decisionmaking. And don't simply take over someone else's solutions and make them your own. Be prepared to forge your own path. You'll be glad you did.

3

Formulating Guidelines

Once you decide to move forward with plans to design a program to help those who are grieving as they face the holidays without the one they love, you will be faced with making a number of decisions about the shape of that event. Many of those decisions will have obvious consequences regarding the people you attract and the nature and scope of the event you sponsor. Other of those decisions will affect only subtly what happens that day. But it's important to make each decision carefully so that all your plans will form a cohesive whole.

It will help for you to have some guidelines in place as you begin your decisionmaking. This will simplify and unify your planning process as well as help assure a well-run program that meets the needs you uncover.

Following are examples of guidelines which have influenced the planning of various holiday events in the past. They were formulated for specific situations and are not meant to be universally applied. If you're going to plan a program for a smaller group of people, or for the members of an existing group or organization, some of these guidelines will not be appropriate for you. In that case you will want to formulate other ones instead. The list that follows is designed to help you start your thinking, not stop it.

Do what you can to make it easy for grieving people to attend.

It requires real effort for people who are grieving to take the step of attending a program like the one you're designing. Their energy level is already low. So probably is their self-esteem. They may feel self-conscious, awkward, out of place. They may not know anyone else who is present, compounding their sense of loneliness. They will not know exactly what the day holds for them or what will be required of them. They may be concerned about keeping their emotions in check. It's possible the surroundings will be unfamiliar.

You will demonstrate authentic care by making it as easy as possible for participants to join you. Make all information about your event clear and concise, including directions on how to get there. Post a telephone number so people can call with their questions beforehand, and there *will* be questions.

Can you make sure parking is convenient? Will your audience prefer to arrive and depart during daytime hours rather than after dark? Will your signage show people where to enter the building and how to proceed to the right room? Will you arrange for hosts to greet and assist them?

Suppose someone says, "My friend is willing to bring me, but she isn't grieving herself. May she come?" What will your answer be? If someone says, "I think I'd like to come but I won't know until the last minute if I'll feel up to it," how will you respond? If someone announces, "I want to come to this one part of your program but not that other part," what will you say?

There is great value in removing as many barriers as possible for people to attend as they wish, to stay as long as feels right, and to leave when they feel they must.

*Do what you can to make people comfortable
once the program begins.*

Show your attendees that you have given thought to their wishes and needs. They deserve relaxing, pleasing surroundings. How can you provide that? They deserve seating that is comfortable and not too close. Rooms should be well-lit and neither too warm nor too cool. Participants should be able to hear all that is said without straining and see all that is presented without having to move.

In other words, one of your roles is to see to it that thoughtful hospitality is practiced in every way imaginable. Considerate touches like ready-made name tags, conveniently-placed boxes of tissues, and light refreshments can quietly demonstrate that people's needs have been thought about and looked after. When people feel they're welcome guests, they're more likely to open up and be themselves. And the more your participants can do that, the more they can chip away at the grieving that is theirs alone to do.

Plan for the whole person.

Grief is more than a psychological response. It affects the mind, the body, the heart, and the soul all at the same time. This will have ramifications for how you design your event. How much will you emphasize people's intellectual capacities and how will you do that? What kinds of words will you use and how many of them? In what ways will you give voice to their spiritual yearnings? Will silence have a place? Music? Some form of inspiration? Will there be ways they can connect with their bodies, or learn more about their physical response to grief, or find ways to care for that bodily aspect of who they are? What will they learn about their feelings and the expression of those feelings? Will there be a way for people's feelings to come out if they wish it? How will their social needs be affirmed?

Many are the possibilities, if you plan for them.

Plan for families as well as individuals.

Grief is a very personal response to loss. It arises out of the close relationship between two human beings—one who has died and one who has survived. Because it is such an individual reaction, it makes sense to concentrate on helping grievers one at a time.

Yet grief also calls for an *interpersonal* response as well. A death commonly touches several people at once, and often many people at once. It affects entire families, whole networks of friends, and sometimes the larger community. That will be something to keep in mind when you're planning your event.

Will you encourage families as well as individuals to attend? Will your literature make that clear? Will your accommodations allow families to sit together? Will your sessions address family issues as well as personal ones?

Families often include children. Will these smaller ones be invited and prepared for? It's clear that children can grieve when they're quite young, even when they're toddlers and certainly by the time they're ready for school. But they grieve in different ways than adults do. They have different questions, different needs, and different ways of responding. Will your program take them into account as well? If so, what will that say about the kind of seating your provide, the kind of workshops you might offer, the kind of remembrance activities you plan, and the kind of professional expertise you draw upon for that day's leadership?

Including children in your activities may alter your plans and stretch your creative thinking. But don't forget that children grieve just as naturally as anyone else. If they're not included in the process, there's a danger their grief won't be recognized and they'll be forgotten mourners.

Plan for men and women alike.

It's almost inevitable you'll have more women than men at your event, for a couple of reasons. Women have longer life expectancies, so there are many more widows than widowers. Another factor is the way people deal with their grief. It's inaccurate to stereotype the way all men and all women grieve. But there is some indication that women are more likely to want to talk with others about their grief, whereas men are more inclined to keep to themselves, thinking it's their responsibility to handle this on their own. Men may wish to make more active responses to their grief, by accomplishing something or building something. Men may also respond more intellectually, whereas women may be freer to approach their grief more emotionally.

A case in point is support groups. Having spoken before many groups of professional caregivers throughout North America, I have often asked for a show of hands of people who are presently leading grief support groups. Then I ask how many of those leaders have more women than men in their groups. Almost all the hands stay up. Then I ask how many have equal numbers of men and women. Sometimes there's a hand or two, sometimes not. Then I ask how many have more men than women in their groups and there's never a hand to be seen. Well, almost never. Once there was a man whose hand shot into the air, indicating he had more men than women in his groups. Surprised, I asked him his secret. He began, "You see, I'm a psychologist who works in a penitentiary..."

If you're not planning to hold your event in a penitentiary, you'll have more women than men in your audience. You'll want to plan for them. But what can you do to meet the needs of the men who attend, both younger men and older men? What might that mean about the subjects of any workshops you offer? Will you make it possible for men to meet and discuss among themselves? Will there be figures in leadership with whom men can identify? Will the masculine way of grieving be as affirmed as well as the more commonly-accepted feminine way?

Plan with the primacy of your intended audience's needs in mind.

Healthy, open, non-manipulative leadership is key. The focus should be on what will aid your attendees rather than what will flatter you or serve your speakers. The overall purpose for the day should drive the decisions you make from start to finish. When you're done, check to see how well you've lived up to this commitment.

Plan with an openness about faith.

The subject of faith cannot be ignored. It's a part of the holiday season. In fact, it's the *basis* of the holiday season. Whether or not one actively practices their religious belief, faith is always there in the background. And there's something about the experience of grief that often brings one's spiritual nature to the fore, no matter what one's religious history. At the same time, however, there can be problems trying to incorporate people's faith understandings in events like these.

If yours is to be a community-wide event for people of all faith systems, you dare not emphasize one religion more than another. That will mean you'll want to monitor the language that's used at your event. You'll do well to use "congregation" rather than "church," for instance, and "the holidays" rather than "Christmas." Or perhaps you'll say "Hannakuh" as often as you say "Christmas." You'll also want to be sensitive and inclusive about the holiday symbols and rituals you discuss and any remembrance ceremonies you plan.

It will also be wise to acknowledge the vast differences in people's belief systems. That includes their ideas about dying and death, about what happens to people after they die, and the kind of relationship that is still possible after a loved one dies physically. It's important to remember that people can be fragile and vulnerable when they're deep in their grief. One must be careful not to impose one's own subjective ideas upon them.

Of course, you may wish to design your holiday event with a particular religion or a specific congregation in mind.

That can be a laudable goal. Just make sure that's clear in your publicity. Then design a day in keeping with that religious perspective, knowing it can be a tremendous help those who are searching for that sort of answer.

Plan with a sensitivity for the unique situation of grieving individuals.

People in grief may be preoccupied with what has happened to them. Their attention spans may be short. Their thinking may be cloudy. What might that mean for your overall design?

They may seem sad and depressed. They may be very low on energy. They may act hesitant and afraid. What will that mean for you?

Their grief may come out in unpredictable ways: gentle tears, loud sobbing, quick anger, unusual quietness. What can you do to be prepared?

They may feel like telling their story in great detail. They may try to monopolize the floor. They may come with a myriad of questions, expecting specific answers. What will you do?

People who are grieving are often not quite themselves. Their memory may be faulty. Their confidence may be a bit shaky. They may have trouble making decisions. Attending this event may open up old wounds or bring back strong feelings they thought they had left behind. What might you do to take these changes into account, without presuming all people in mourning are like that, and also without condescending to them?

Provide answers, within reason.

Many times those who are grieving have never known serious loss before. The experience of grief may be alien to them. Or they may have forgotten what it's like. With so

24

few answers provided by the culture around them, or surrounded by conflicting messages, they may be on a desperate search for vital information. How long does grief last? What are its stages? How do I know what's normal and abnormal? What if I feel I don't want to go on living?

Those who choose to attend this particular event are also looking for information about living through the days ahead, at a time when people around them seem so happy and when so many fond memories come to the surface. How should they celebrate this year? Or should they celebrate at all? What will help the blues?

Your participants will be looking for concrete ideas and specific solutions, both during your event and after it ends. What will you do? How will you respond to their requests for answers, realizing that answers are not always available?

Offer hope.

As much as anything, most people want to know this grief will eventually end and they'll feel better again. They want to believe something positive can come from all this. They want to have something to hold on to. Do you have something to offer them that is honest and real, encouraging and true? What is it? How will you make it known?

Guidelines akin to these and guidelines you create on your own will help you focus your thinking as you prepare to formulate your plans.

4

Designing What You'll Do

Chances are you'll have more ideas to ponder, more decisions to make, and more preparations to oversee than you first thought. A well-planned event will requite a solid investment of time and effort. But it's exactly that: an investment. And it will pay real dividends, sooner as well as later.

You'll face various decisions as you begin your planning process. Take the time you need to consider the options, evaluate the advantages and disadvantages, and assess your resources. Remain open to your possibilities.

The Planning Group

It's essentially impossible to start a well-designed, smoothly-run program entirely by yourself. Some things you cannot know. Some skills you do not have. Some tasks you cannot do. And even if you *could* do it all yourself, you would be limiting the success of your event by not including others in the process. Involving other people in planning and leading these events spreads personal ownership and harnesses more available energy. It increases the likelihood you'll have covered all—or at least more—of your bases beforehand. It will unleash the greater power of creative thinking that can occur when people build on one another's ideas. Ultimately, it will increase the chances that you'll design an event that will really suit the needs of the people you want to serve. While this coordination will take work, it will decrease the labor that one person or a handful of people must expend. It will also help guard against this event becoming closely identified with just one leader.

Organize a steering committee that will be in charge of what happens. If your event is to be identified with a single organization, congregation, or business, your committee may be small and confined to your membership or your employees. If your base of support and your audience appeal is to be broader in nature, it will be important for varied backgrounds, abilities, interests, and connections to be represented on your committee. Professionals you might seek include:

• Bereavement counselors
• Assorted mental health professionals, including psychologists, social workers, and school counselors
• Representatives of social service agencies
• Representatives of existing grief-related groups, like Compassionate Friends, Mothers Against Drunk Driving, Widow-to-Widow, etc.
• Clergy
• Funeral directors

Depending upon the scope of your plans, you might invite people who are knowledgeable about fund-raising and marketing. It's also important that the voice of the bereaved be heard. Consider including one or two individuals who have a special interest in a program like this because of what has happened in their life. Or if you're choosing between a psychologist who has experienced grief firsthand and one who hasn't, for instance, it might be wise to choose the former.

Make your invitation clear, whether you do it in person, by telephone, or with a letter. Explain what this group will do. Estimate the amount of time it might take so there are no surprises. Explain why you're asking that person, including describing the specific strengths you believe they will bring to this endeavor. Describe the good that can come from this type event. Give people time to think about their response if they wish. If they decline your invitation and you feel their participation is critical, ask if they would agree to participate in a more limited way. You might develop an advisory committee which would meet just once or twice to give general, informal direction. Or maybe they would agree to be an individual advisor. Such people can lend credibility to what you want to do. They are also more likely to step forward for specific requests if you need them, like leading a workshop or underwriting a certain expense. And they can always help spread the word about this exciting program.

If someone says "no," another option is to ask them to recommend someone else who might be willing to serve in a similar capacity. Their ideas may be better than your own. If you're given such a name, ask if you can mention who it was who recommended them.

There is no magic number for the size of this steering committee. It will probably take at least three or four people. Six or eight members is a workable size. Once you get beyond ten or twelve, however, your group may become too large. It will be difficult to find a convenient time for everyone to meet. Decisionmaking may become unnecessarily complicated. In addition, responsibilities may be spread too thin.

The Initial Planning

Once your planning committee is in place, call the first meeting. You have several options for determining the leadership of your sessions. You might elect a leader or co-leaders. You might ask one person experienced at group dynamics to guide the meetings, more as a facilitator than as a leader. Some groups have tried rotating leadership at each meeting. Others have presumed that the person or persons active in forming the committee will conduct these meetings, making sure the power remains with the committee and not with the convener.

Meet regularly and as needed. Meetings of sixty to ninety minutes tend to be most effective. Meetings that go longer than two hours tend to have diminishing returns. It may also be difficult to justify that commitment of time from the kind of people you'd like to attract to your group— they're likely to be involved in other pursuits too.

Be sure you allow enough time for your committee to work. Plan on at least three or four months lead time to do all that needs to be done. Six months is much better. Better still is to work a year in advance. While your actual work will be limited when your program is still twelve months away, you can make important decisions in a timely fashion which will allow later decisions to fall into place more easily and help you avoid unnecessary schedule conflicts.

Divide into subgroups for specific, between-session tasks. Give each subgroup the opportunity to report fully on all their work. Keep decisionmaking within the larger committee as much as possible so that various plans do not conflict with one another. Do your official business as a committee and use your time together wisely. But that doesn't mean you can't have fun together in your meetings. Group members can banter back and forth or find humor in their relationships and still function quite effectively and efficiently.

Among your first decisions will be the overall focus of your day. What exactly do you want to offer those who will attend? Specific ideas for getting through the approaching holidays will presumably be high on your agenda. How much information will you provide? How will you provide it? Will one person or more than one person speak? Will this be one-way communication or will you encourage interaction? Will you provide information about grief in general? What about other matters that grieving people might want to know? Will you foster any other kinds of activities for those who attend? Will you somehow memorialize those who have died? Will there be moments of inspiration? Will you serve refreshments or a meal? The structure for your day begins here.

The Name

Whatever you plan and whatever its scope, give your program a title. Create a name. This will help communicate to your prospective participants what will be happening that day. It will also allow you to frame the event in your own way, placing what you have to offer in an affirming light.

Be clear with your wording. People won't attend if they don't know what they're getting into. That is especially true of the newly bereaved who will be hesitant to tackle a new undertaking if it feels foreign or threatening.

Consider naming the event concisely with two, three, or four words, followed by a subtitle that will further define your event. Here's one example: "Growing Through Grief: How To Make It Through The Holidays When You're Bereaved." Here's another: "Handling Holiday Grief: A Day of Support and Remembrance for the Recently Bereaved." Be creative with your ideas, but don't get "cutesy." This is a heavy time in people's lives and they will appreciate your taking their feelings seriously. And don't promise more than you can deliver with your title. This holiday will not be like previous holidays for those who are grieving. It will not contain the same joy. It cannot be made easy. The name you give your event should be sensitive to that realization.

You might create more than just a name. If you can call upon the assistance of a graphic artist, you might design a logo for your event. By placing this design on all your printed materials and by using it in all your marketing efforts, you'll help people remember what you're doing and build the impression that something of quality is being prepared for them. Don't attempt a logo, however, without the services of a graphic artist. Amateurs often do not understand what makes for effective visual symbols. If you're not careful, this distinctive touch which was meant to enhance the image of your day will take away from it. Better to have no logo at all than one that falls decidedly short.

The Time Frame

The best time to help someone prepare for the holidays, obviously, is before the holidays begin. Your religious heritage will dictate the dates for those days. (Are you aware that "holidays" is actually a simplified version of "holy days"?) In large parts of North America, the holidays in general extend from sometime in November through the first of the year. That means that a good time to schedule your event might be early and middle November. Some groups have had success with later November and even early December. A few have tried the very last of October.

Select a date that best suits the purposes of your group and the people you want to serve. Select it early. People's schedules fill quickly. So do the calendars of other organizations. Check to see if any similar events will be happening nearby or at the same time. Duplication of effort can be wasteful. On the other hand, some communities are large enough and some audiences specific enough that two or more similar events may complement one another and even build on one another.

The kind of event you're planning will help determine which day of the week and what time of day you'll choose. If your schedule calls for more than a couple of hours of activities, you'll probably meet on a Saturday or Sunday. Some groups have chosen an all-day Saturday format. Others have selected a morning or afternoon on either Saturday or Sunday. Services of commemoration that stand by themselves and last only an hour or two are usually held in the evening or on a Sunday afternoon. A few groups have been more ambitious by planning a weekend retreat.

Another option is to plan a series of events—two, three or four meetings that take place both before the holidays begin and as they unfold. Usually there's a different theme for each meeting.

The Focus

The purpose you have set for your event will dictate how much time you will spend doing what. Many are the directions you may choose to go. Do what seems most appropriate for your intended audience and for the resources at your disposal. Then do it as well as you can and as thoughtfully as you're able. Keep in mind that the bereaved are not all alike. Widows or widowers with young children face different issues and different holiday patterns than the elderly who live alone. Parents who have lost a child to cancer or SIDS may approach the day one way, while an adolescent whose parent has committed suicide will approach it another way, and they'll each be asking their own unique questions.

The Schedule

If your focus is more concentrated, a gathering lasting one to two hours may suffice. If you're planning an event to last either a half day or full day, keep the following in mind:

Provide for large group input earlier in the day and plan for more interactive activities later in the time together. This will give people opportunity first to develop some common bases for reference and understanding. It will also assist people to move into this experience gradually. People who are grieving often want to "test the waters" carefully before revealing much about themselves.

Allow opportunities for people to connect with one another. Plan rest breaks that are often enough and long enough to facilitate conversation. Find ways to stimulate group and personal interaction.

Allow people to move in and out of their grief. Some moments will be serious, without question. But can lighter or more joyful moments be planned without disturbing the flow of the day while still honoring people's feelings?

Presume that people will stay for the entire event, but be understanding if people leave early. Some bereaved feel threatened by the display of emotions, whether it's their own or others'. Some will be more ready to process what has happened and is happening to them.

No single activity should last longer than 90 minutes.

The Cost

You must decide if there will be a cost for your event, and if there is to be one, what it will be. There are valid reasons to decide either way.

Events of this sort generally do not require a large amount of funding. Volunteers will do some or all of the work. Meeting space may be available at little or no expense. Supplies may be negligible. Printing and marketing costs can mount up, but these are also the expenses that are most likely to be donated. If it's your business or organization that's sponsoring this event, you may elect to underwrite all expenses from your own funds as a part of your mission or outreach to others. Or you may search for other sorts of funding to offset your expenses. You can then offer this program free of charge to whoever wishes to attend.

A second way to proceed is to charge a nominal amount to cover some or all of your costs. Some groups have instituted registration fees of $3, $5, and even $10, depending upon the length of the program, whether or not a meal is served, and the costs associated with renting facilities and bringing in a featured speaker. People usually do not mind paying for something they perceive has value. Many people even prefer to do so. This can also be a way of developing commitment from your participants.

There is something to be said for offering your program at no expense as a holiday gesture in itself—a gift one wishes to give another. Consequently, this appears to be the way most preparing-for-the-holidays events are handled. Even when expenses are substantial, you can generally find businesses, foundations, and philanthropic organizations that are willing to support such a worthy and thoughtful program. In that case, unless the donor requests otherwise, you'll want to acknowledge these contributions, both privately and publicly, being careful not to turn this appreciation into any sort of advertisement or endorsement.

The Location

The decision about your site may be a given. It may be your sanctuary or fellowship hall if yours is a congregation sponsoring this event, or a chapel if yours is a funeral home. In other cases, your planning committee will need to select an appropriate site. Your program will help dictate your options. Do you need one room or several rooms? Flexible or fixed seating? A place for informal gathering and refreshments or not? A public address system? Is cost a factor?

You'll want to keep the following in mind:

• Disabled accessibility is a must.

• Security and lighted parking are important to many people, especially the kind of people who will be attending your event.

• The choice of site may also be influenced by community perceptions. Certain religious institutions or social service agencies, for instance, may have a reputation for being either inclusive or exclusive in a given community. Even if you're only borrowing or renting facilities, you may be discouraging or encouraging participation based upon other events that have taken place, or have not taken place, at that particular location.

The Amenities

Refreshments encourage people to mingle, to take their time, and to talk with one another. It also gives people something to do if they're feeling uneasy or nervous. Donations of this sort are usually easy to come by. If yours is an all-day event, you'll have to decide if a meal will be provided or if you'll send people out to nearby restaurants. While the latter approach is easier for your steering group to plan, your participants will probably appreciate being able to eat together and talk about their common concerns or whatever they wish. A common meal adds to the sense of community too.

The amenity of strategically-placed boxes of tissues has already been discussed. Pencils or pens and note paper or notepads will be a nice touch for those who forgot to bring writing materials or those who didn't realize they'd want to preserve so many ideas.

Name tags are important if you want people to interact with one another. Handouts may help: a folder, an agenda, a listing of helpful resources, perhaps a reprint of a good article or two. One sheet might highlight your donors.

A gesture that is always well received is the giving away of a book or booklet on the subject of getting through the holidays when you're bereaved. Such writings can often be ordered in quantity at attractive discounts.

The Follow-up

Your event does not have to end with the conclusion of your last planned activity of the day. You may want to make it convenient for people to connect with one another in the future. A sign-up sheet for those who wish to talk with others who have experienced a similar loss may lead to future meetings. You might help put in place a "buddy system" for those who wish it—a way for people to talk with one another regularly, including when they're having especially trying times.

You might use your registrations to develop a mailing list to keep in touch during the coming year, for additional specialized activities, or for information about next year's program. You may wish to help organize a Thanksgiving or Christmas Day meal or a Hannakuh or New Year's Eve gathering for those who find themselves alone.

Another form of follow-up is an evaluation form which can be completed by all attendees. These can be invaluable in planning your future events. It can be a part of your packet of handouts.

The first and most important step is to put together a planning committee of dedicated, talented people. Go for people who are sensitive and caring, energetic and creative. Fashion a mix of those who like to be detail-oriented and those who are visionaries. Give them the authority they need, then set them loose. They'll do a great piece of work.

5

Planning Informational Components

It's important to provide a certain amount of information that will help usher the recently bereaved through the turmoil of the upcoming holidays. If your event is planned as mainly a memorialization of the lives of those who have died, the information you make available may be limited to the take-home materials you provide, the books you make available, and the personal conversations you make time for.

If yours is a longer event, however, or if you wish to emphasize the educational possibilities of your time together, you'll want to provide information in other ways too.

Large Group Presentation

If you're planning an event that's at least several hours long, a good way to begin is to gather your entire group in one room for a presentation which will set the theme for your time together. This will allow you to officially welcome your attendees, help them feel at home, and give structure to the time ahead. This can be an excellent time to get right to what brought them to your gathering: the questions and concerns they have about handling their grief during the upcoming holiday period.

It's worth addressing either or both of two major themes. One subject, naturally, is guidance in how to proceed through the coming holidays with as much health and hope as possible while still missing terribly the one who has died. It's an appropriate time to validate the strong emotions grieving people are likely to feel, to acknowledge the stressful situation in which they find themselves, and to offer general insights and perhaps specific ideas for making it through the coming weeks.

Thirty to sixty minutes is a good length for a presentation of this sort. You might call upon a person who is comfortable and accomplished in public speaking as well as acquainted with the subject at hand. An experienced bereavement counselor or psychologist, a knowledgeable teacher or professor, a sensitive clergyperson or funeral director might serve in this capacity. Perhaps there's someone in your community who knows firsthand what holiday grief is like and is prepared to help educate others. Maybe you can locate someone who's written about it. Some groups bring in speakers from outside their community who do this sort of work professionally.

It's best if this presentation offers help and hope without prescribing exactly what bereaved people should do or not do over the holiday period. The uniqueness of each individual and family should always be respected. People will usually appreciate being given options from which they can choose or general guidelines they can customize and build upon. Often people will be satisfied if they can take away a handful of ideas to try or a couple assurances they can cling to when they need them most. One assurance that often helps, for instance, and a proven one, is the fact that living through the actual holiday itself is not as difficult as most people imagine it will be. Worrying about the time is worse than living through it. Such knowledge can help ease people's minds.

Stories maintain people's attention. So do actual examples of what other people have chosen to do as a way of honoring their loved ones while still celebrating the season. People will benefit from learning more than just particular rituals they can try or alternative ways they can handle traditional gift-giving. They will appreciate receiving a few clues for dealing with those people who don't understand how deep their grief goes, for instance, or how they can take especially good care of themselves in the weeks and months ahead.

Another possibility is to feature a panel discussion. Your panel might be comprised either of informed professionals or of experienced individuals, whatever their professional background, who are authorities on grief because they've lived through it. Or your panel might contain both sorts of people. This presentation might be scheduled directly after your main speaker or in place of a main speaker. Pay special attention to the person who will moderate your panel discussion. They should be adept at keeping dialogue moving, facilitating differences of opinion, and eliciting questions and responses from the audience. Any words from the floor should be repeated for everyone to hear if a microphone cannot be made available. Sometimes audiovisual presentations can aid in educating your participants.

A second useful topic to begin your event is the whole subject of grief itself. Today many people don't understand the workings of grief or what to expect of it, since it's not ingrained in our culture in the way it once was. When the process of grief is explained and normalized, people often feel relieved and gratified. If you begin with this sort of a program, it's probably best to include some "holiday helps" later, either as the second half of this talk or as the subject of a follow-up presentation. Some groups have used this topic as the last event of the day, just before people depart.

The format of your program and the limits of your schedule will determine whether or not you include a time for questions and answers. The larger your audience, the more cumbersome that procedure may become. Yet don't forget what adult learners are like. They're determined. They want clear explanations and concrete answers. Often they prefer the voice of experience and of wisdom to the recitation of facts and figures, no matter how current. They don't want to be read to. And they want to know what *works*, not just what's interesting.

Unless you've intentionally narrowed your audience by the way you've marketed your program, all information that's supplied to the whole group should be geared to the general interests of most grievers. This is not the place to give inordinate attention to the issues only suicide survivors face or to concentrate on how families with young children best celebrate the holidays. More specialized information is best offered other ways. Remarks should be aimed at men and women alike, both the older and the younger, from various backgrounds and with varied lifestyles.

While you may expect to attract the *recently* bereaved to your event, remember you may have people in your audience who are mourning a death that occurred years ago, and perhaps *many* years ago. Any death is likely to bring former deaths into one's awareness. Moreover, sometimes people come to realize they have not yet fully mourned a particular death from long before, whether or not they experienced a recent loss. They may then choose to begin their way through the grieving process as they could not before, having learned it's never too late to do so.

Small Group Workshops

If you've designed your event to allow for other sorts of educational opportunities, a series of workshops may serve your purposes well. By this means, you make it possible for people to learn more about those specific issues and skills they're most interested in. You encourage freer group discussion and easier personal interaction. You give people the chance to stretch, move around, and refresh themselves. You make for a more varied, interesting, and personalized experience.

The number and kind of workshops you offer will

depend on several factors:

- What do you believe your participants want to learn?
- How diverse do you expect your group to be?
- What are the interests and abilities of your potential workshop leaders?
- How much room is available?
- How much time do you have?
- How many total participants do you expect?

A rule of thumb is to plan a workshop for every fifteen to twenty people in attendance. That will allow you to have thirty or forty people in some sessions and only five or ten in others. Some workshops do well with larger numbers, others with smaller numbers, so don't standardize their size. Remember also that once you have many more than about forty people in attendance, it's no longer a workshop—it's another lecture. If one workshop is especially popular, trying repeating it, or schedule two different sessions of the same workshop simultaneously.

An hour or so is a good workshop length. Anything less than forty-five or fifty minutes does not allow time for a complete presentation of a topic. Anything much longer than an hour and a quarter will become taxing for your participants. If you schedule one workshop period, sixty to seventy-five minutes is an appropriate time period, with ninety minutes as an absolute maximum. If you have two or more workshop periods, sixty minutes is probably a good maximum, with plenty of time for people to move at their leisure from one room to another.

Create your own smorgasbord of opportunities. The following workshop subjects may help start your thinking.

- *The nature and process of grief.*

Think of this as a mini-course in Grief 101. What is grief? How does it work? What's to be expected? What helps and doesn't help? How does one know when complications develop? People who choose this workshop will appreciate having plenty of time to pose their questions; the people who attend your event will be hungry for information. Look for a trained professional to lead this workshop, someone who's current with the latest research. Avoid supplying simplistic answers about predictable "stages of grief" or precise time periods. Several excellent videotapes about the grief process are on the market. Check around.

• *How children grieve and what adults can do to help.*

Parents often have many questions and concerns about their children when a significant death shakes up their family life. Since children have only limited ability to conceptualize death and afterlife, and since they express themselves differently than adults do, the grief of young people can appear unusual, or it may be hard to see at all. Teach parents how children respond to death and grief at various ages. Explain how adults best talk with children. Give examples. Show what parental figures can do to help in addition to talking. Offer a detailed bibliography of good children's books. Ask a school counselor, child psychologist, classroom teacher, or a leader of children's support groups to conduct this workshop.

• *How adolescents grieve and what adults can do to help.*

Adolescents grieve more like adults than children, but they still have their special issues and unique ways. There's something contradictory about adolescence and grief. Teenagers are programmed to start breaking away from their families as they begin to develop their individuality and independence. Grief has the opposite effect—it calls for families to unite and draw closer. An option is to combine adolescent grief in the same workshop with children's grief.

• *How grief affects whole families.*

An expert in the psychology of family systems could help participants understand how grief disrupts family life and what can be done to facilitate the process of a gradual return to a more normal life together. This could be designed just for parents or parental figures, or for entire families to attend.

- *How men and women grieve differently.*

People often want to understand how it is men tend to respond to grief in one way, while women take a little different approach. It's critical to resist stereotypical thinking, but it's worth looking at some of the possible causes and effects, realizing some men will grieve in a more "feminine" way and vice versa. An alternative workshop might be one for just men to attend, where they can express themselves, learn a little about masculine psychology, and be affirmed in their own natural ways. Such a workshop should be led by a male.

- *When your child dies.*

Bereaved parents often deal with issues other mourners do not, including the fact that children are not supposed to die before their parents. The death of a child may cause increased feelings of helplessness, guilt, and anger. Grief may last longer. Group discussion and interaction can help struggling families, especially when the workshop leader has had experience in working with this kind of grief. Remember that some attendees may be the parents of *adult* children who have died. Might this call for a separate workshop? Remember also that stillbirths and other neonatal deaths require full grief responses. The depth of such losses are often not fully appreciated by others. Still another workshop possibility?

- *When your spouse or mate dies.*

Spousal bereavement has its own characteristics. This loss can set in motion a series of other losses that have far-reaching effects: the loss of income, loss of residence, and loss of friendships, to give only a few examples. It can raise troublesome questions involving identity, sexuality, and life meaning. Might you have separate workshops for the younger widowed and the older widowed?

43

- *When you're the survivor of suicide.*

Not surprisingly, people mourning the death of someone who has intentionally taken their life usually have complex issues to work through. The stigma of this kind of death can make it more difficult for them to receive the support they need. This workshop will require very qualified leadership.

- *How to manage transition in your life.*

Every grief due to the death of someone close requires the making of a transition, but not all transitions are related to the grief of death. Learning about the normal, rather predictable processes of all human transitions can help navigate this difficult time. It helps to know the proactive steps one can take.

- *How to manage stress.*

Grieving people are often looking for ways to control their stress levels. A number of procedures can help. This workshop might feature some techniques participants can try on the spot. Recommended books and articles will help.

- *How to meditate.*

At a time when significant life issues are more likely to surface and life stresses increase, the practice of meditation can help bring stability and serenity to daily life. An experienced leader can describe the possibilities, do some basic training, and show ways to expand one's abilities. Learning new ways to pray might be a part of this workshop, or its own topic. Learning yoga is another possibility. The use of relaxation and guided imagery is still another.

- *The value of journaling and how to do it.*

Journal-keeping is an excellent catharsis for grieving people. It can give them a needed distance and perspective. It can preserve their thoughts and feelings for later reflection and discovery. In short, it can help them heal. The principles of journaling are simple, the results proven. The workshop might also demonstrate how people can write the story of their loss in other ways: as short story, biography, autobiography, or poetry.

• *How to help someone who's grieving.*

If you want to attract attendees eager to learn how to do what's best for friends, family, and others, this might be a worthwhile addition to your offerings. Sometimes it helps as much for people to realize what *not* to do.

• *How to help grieving people in your congregation.*

If you encourage professional participation, this workshop is a natural. Congregations are ideally suited to do bereavement ministry—it's just they're usually not sure how to proceed. Some helpful books and articles have been written.

• *Homemaker skills for the widowed.*

You might have the makings for a single workshop here, or separate workshops for widows and widowers, or workshops focused on various topics. Some widowers may find themselves in the dark about cooking for themselves and doing household chores they've never done before, just as certain widows may wonder about the basics of auto maintenance and simple home repair. This information may seem rudimentary but it can make a major difference in some people's lives.

• *Dealing with finances after a death.*

The death of a close family member, especially a spouse, can create a number of unusual financial situations with which one has had no experience. What should be done with insurance death benefits, legal settlements, and other matters relating to the deceased person's estate and one's own future? What does estate planning mean anyway? The leader of this workshop should be a trusted, unbiased professional without any conflicts of interest.

• *Bibliotherapy for the bereaved.*

A bereavement professional, interested librarian, or avid reader could offer a rundown of books to help someone in grief, by topic: grief in general, instructive life stories, inspirational writings, help for specific kinds of death, etc. Resources could include magazines, audiotapes, videotapes, and movies.

• *Developing new holiday rituals.*

What are the rituals others have employed which have helped them? What can be learned from other customs and traditions?

There are many other options. What about a workshop for developing an exercise program or learning self-defense techniques? Tai chi? Coping with loneliness? Being a good caregiver? Exploring the mind/body connection? Discovering the meaning of your dreams? Locating grief-related resources on the internet?

Ask grieving people what they want to learn. Ask others what they're prepared to teach. Then develop an interesting, well-rounded program.

If you want to welcome families of all ages, provide child care for the very young and include workshops designed just for children and adolescents.

Consider assigning a host/facilitator to each workshop as well as a leader. This person can make introductions, watch the clock, deal with any mechanics relating to the room, supplies, and equipment, and relate to the participants informally.

Give each workshop an inviting title. Don't use "The Nature and Process of Grief." Make it something like "Everything You Ever Wanted to Know About Grief" or "The Ten Principles of Healthy Grieving" or "Grief: How It Works and What You Can Do." Include a one- or two-line description with each title so people have some idea what they'll learn and how they'll learn it. Include leaders' names. If there's room to add their title or affiliation, do so.

It may be easier to sign up leaders than you expect.

Yours is a worthy cause. Many people will feel pleased you've turned to them when you might have asked someone else. In some cases they may recognize subtle benefits in being identified with your program. If you're having difficulty finding someone to agree to lead a particular session, try asking two co-leaders, spreading out the responsibility.

Concurrent Small Group Experiences

There's another way to encourage small group participation rather than using various workshops. That's to divide your participants into small groups following your keynote presentation and lead them to discuss with one another and learn from each other. If you choose this approach, plan on assigning a facilitator to each group—someone who's skilled at leading discussion and encouraging participation. This format is more likely to be appropriate if most people know one another somehow, however slightly. These should not be treated as support groups; they're discussion groups.

Miscellaneous Thoughts

• People often like to take information home with them so they can digest it at their own speed and so they can preserve thoughts, names, addresses, titles, etc. Many of them will be grateful for any handouts you provide.

• People may not know about all the community resources at their disposal, including groups that serve particular grief-related needs. Might you provide a display area where tables and booths could be set up?

• People like to browse tables where books and other resources are for sale. Might someone on your steering committee oversee this function? One option is for you to set up your own little bookstore, with any profits subsidizing the costs of your event. Another option is to ask another group to do that as their own moneymaker. A service-minded bookstore might prepare an on-site booth, complete with cash register and a credit card machine.

• Many people like to learn from one another. Encourage interaction among participants with the schedule you develop, the places where people can meet and converse, and the way you lay out your rooms. Instead of having everyone sit in straight rows facing one end of a room, perhaps you can arrange for some groups to sit in circles, or semi-circles, or facing one another. Some people even like to sit on pillows on the floor.

• People who are grieving often want to talk. Let them. Some may want to be quiet. Let them. Some may wish to have a private room where they can go if they'd like to talk confidentially with someone. Might you arrange for such a place and such a person?

6

Planning A Commemoration

Your event may be designed solely as a time of remembrance and commemoration, or you may elect to make such a ritual just one part of what you offer your participants. There is real value, however you do it, in making sure that your attendees are offered a carefully-planned ceremony to ritually remember those who have died. It's also helpful to design this ritual so it will honor and encourage the bereaved as well.

The Nature and Value of Ritual

A ritual is an outward gesture or action that expresses, often symbolically, an inner human reality. This reality can include what one thinks and feels about the present as well as the future.

Whether it's very short and simple or longer and more elaborate, a ritual can be a powerful means of dealing with significant life transitions. It can help give expression to what's happening at a critical juncture of a person's or a family's life, whether that's expressed alone or in a group. When words are used, it can name what's difficult to name. When symbolic actions are used, it can help give expression to what goes deeper than words can convey at that moment.

One aspect of rituals—and an important aspect of commemoration rituals at holiday times—is that they do more than help people own up to what has happened to them and to where they are in life. Rituals in and of themselves can help people take a step forward. They do not just *describe* a transition—they *are* a transition, or at least one part of that transition. Such rituals not only suggest that healing is possible, but they act as healing agents, fostering growth in themselves.

The Purpose of Ritual

In their book *Rituals for Our Times*, Evan Imler-Black and Janine Roberts suggest that rituals can serve any of five purposes:

• For *relating*. Rituals help people understand and express something about their relationships with other people, both living and dead. They can also be used to help maintain those relationships.

• For *changing*. By offering the use of established, accepted, and natural symbols and actions, rituals can help make various human transitions, even traumatic ones, more manageable and safe.

• For *healing*. Following a time of trauma or loss, rituals can help people move toward health and wholeness. In being given opportunities to experience and express empathy, compassion, and forgiveness, people can grow in openness and self-acceptance.

• For *believing*. Rituals offer the chance for deeply-held beliefs to be clarified and stated, whether those beliefs are corporate and universal or more private and individual. They help people make meaning of significant life experiences.

• For *celebrating*. Life cycle rituals like weddings, graduations, birthdays, and anniversaries create opportunities for family and friends to affirm and communicate their joy, as well as to honor the richness of these life experiences. Funerals and other remembrance events also involve celebration, though in a different way. They celebrate a life that was important, a relationship that made a difference, and a love that cannot be taken away.

Note that the commemoration ritual your group might

design for individuals and families can easily involve not just some but all five of these purposes. Your ceremony can bring people together and encourage them to relate to one another, as well as maintain ties with those who have died. Your ritual can help them both mark and make their transition from who they were before this death to who they are becoming as they mourn their loss and make changes in their life. Your ritual can certainly be an avenue for healing, a time for believing, and an opportunity for celebration in the truest sense of the word.

An earlier ritual, the funeral itself, presuming there was one, will have offered similar purposes to the bereaved families who attend your event. But chances are good many of them will have been in shock during that time; they may not have realized or appreciated all that happened. In this day and age, there are few or no accepted rituals to assist the bereaved through their lengthy mourning process following the funeral. The ritual you design can help mourners express what they feel deep within, realizing that fellow mourners in attendance are feeling something similar, and that other people who gather near them are prepared to honor and validate their loss and grief.

You may find that some participants at your event did not or could not attend the funeral or memorial service for their loved one. They may be looking for this to serve as a substitute.

Planning a Ritual of Commemoration

Your ritual will be best if it's *your* ritual. Gather ideas and writings from other sources, including those who have created these events before you. But put it all together in your own way, taking into account your group's needs as you understand them, your own strengths and abilities as leaders of ritual, the location of the ceremony, the traditions

51

from which your participants come, and any other factors that reveal themselves. Use your head, your heart, and your soul to design what seems appropriate. If there's any question, follow your heart and soul.

If you decide to utilize what other people have written or created, it's appropriate to credit them for their work. But remember that you don't have to use something word-for-word if it doesn't quite fit your circumstances, especially if it's a prayer or responsive reading designed for liturgies like these. Re-work it. Change words here and there. Then credit your source by noting "inspired by…" or "adapted from…". Copyrighted materials, of course, are another matter. Request permission to use them.

Your ritual may be religious in a traditional sense or it may be spiritual in a more holistic sense. Each has its advantages.

A religious service calls upon themes and symbols that are shared by a group as a whole, have brought meaning to life in the past, and offer sanctioned authority. Such a service can include not just the written and spoken word but familiar music, meaningful hymns, and commonly-accepted ritual practices. If your event is intended to attract only members of a certain faith or worshipping community, then by all means utilize the symbols and the traditions that bind such people together.

On the other hand, if your event is designed for the larger community, and if you wish your service of com-memoration to still be religious, consider how you might be inclusive in your design. You might draw leadership from at least two or three major faith traditions: a rabbi, a minister, and a priest, for instance. Or if clergy from only one faith officiates, make sure that prayers, readings, and stories of other traditions are included, and noted as such. Some places are more multicultural than others, but remember there are Muslim, Hindu, Confucian, Baha'i, Sikh, and

Buddhist traditions as well as Jewish and Christian ones.

Another option is to make your service spiritual without making it specifically religious. Professional clergy may officiate, or laity may do so. Readings and stories from certain faith traditions may be used, but so may other readings and resources: writings of respected people of wisdom, poetry from the ages, excerpts from books and plays, perhaps the creations of people involved in planning the service itself, or those attending the service. You might make a point of including the creative inspirations of people of all ages, children as well as adults.

A service of remembrance can be genuinely spiritual without appearing generic. It simply requires careful planning, the use of richly meaningful symbols and resources, and the direction of leaders who communicate and evoke spiritual depth.

The Design of a Service of Commemoration

In broad outline, a service of commemoration may consist of six main parts:

A time of gathering
A time of focusing
A time of reflecting
A time of remembering
A time of integrating
A time of departing

Various other elements may be inserted into this outline, depending upon the wishes of those designing the service and the perceived expectations of those attending the service. Prayers, readings, group singing, a choral presentation, spoken meditations, an audiovisual presentation, liturgical dance, and times of silence and reflection, for instance, may all be incorporated in many different ways.

Some general guidelines and suggestions follow.

The First Part: A Time of Gathering

It's important to somehow separate this period of time from whatever period precedes it. Your goal is to set this time apart, to prepare it as special. The playing of quiet music may help people make the transition from one place to another in their minds, hearts, and souls. Such music can also help people feel quiet inside. It can help them to open to another kind of reality than their everyday life. The options are many: organ, piano, synthesizer, harp, violin, flute, guitar, to name just a few. Perhaps a duo or a small ensemble might play. There's something to be said for the immediacy and the richness of a live performance, but recorded music can also serve this purpose quite well. In some situations, so can silence.

Something more than the sound of music or the sound of silence is needed, however. A spoken greeting, an invitation to make this transition, a responsive reading, a recited poem—or all of these—can serve to gather your audience's attention and help them move into this hallowed time.

Following are a few examples, which may be used in various ways.

Come, let us make love deathless, thou and I,
Seeing that our footing on earth is brief....
                              Herbert Trench

Almighty God, from whence we come, and unto whom our spirits return: Thou hast been our dwelling place in all generations. Thou art our refuge and strength, a very present help in trouble. Grant us thy blessing in this hour, and enable us so to put our trust in Thee that our spirits may grow calm and our hearts be comforted. Lift our eyes beyond the shadows of earth, and help us see the light of eternity.
                              Traditional Christian prayer

There is a time for everything, for all things under the sun: a time to be born and a time to die, a time to laugh and a time to cry, a time to dance and a time to mourn, a time to seek and a time to lose, a time to forget and a time to re-member.

This day in sacred convocation we remember those who gave us life. We remember those who enriched our lives with love and beauty, kindness and compassion, thoughtful-ness and understanding. We renew our bonds to those who have gone the way of all earth. As we reflect upon those whose memory moves us this day, we seek consolation, and the strength and the insight born of faith.

Tender as a parent with a child, the Lord is merciful. God knows how we are fashioned, remembers that we are dust. Our days are as grass; we flourish as a flower in a field. The wind passes over it and is gone, and no one can recognize where it grew. But the Lord's compassion for us, the Lord's righteousness to children's children, remain, age after age, unchanging.

Traditional Jewish prayer

We come together as people drawn to life,
   and yet people acquainted with death.
We come full of our memories—
   those memories that are hard for us to bear,
    those memories that lift us and give us meaning,
     those memories that give us the courage to go on.
We come together today knowing that we are not alone—
   that others struggle even as we struggle,
    that others love even as we have loved, as we love still.
We come together knowing that others hope
   even as we try to hope,
    clinging to the assurances that help us make our way
    from hour to hour, from day to day.
May we find our full share of love and hope
   now in this hour of togetherness.
J.E.M.

Drop thy still dews of quietness,
Till all our strivings cease;
Take from our souls the strain and stress,
And let our ordered lives confess
The beauty of thy peace.

John Greenleaf Whittier

The Second Part: A Time of Focusing

Once this time apart has been demarcated, it's appropriate to prepare people more specifically. What's the purpose of this time that's now beginning? What will be its theme? What will be happening? What won't be happening? One way to do that is with a clear statement of purpose read or spoken by one of the ritual leaders. These words do not need to be especially formal—in fact, they *shouldn't* be, if you want people to feel comfortable and natural. But these words should be prepared in advance, because they set the stage for all that will follow.

Another way is to use a responsive reading, either by itself or following the leader's words. Here's one example:

Leader: We come this day to share with one another our journey through grief and our climb to hope.
People: We come together knowing that we are not alone in our struggles and believing we will not be left empty in our search for renewed life.
Leader: We gather today with questions still in our hearts, with mysteries still enwrapping our souls.
People: We gather as seekers after the truth, wherever truth will lead us, and as pilgrims on the way, wherever our journey takes us.
Leader: We join in this hour, searching for strength for the living of all our days.
People: We join together in faith, in hope, and especially in this way: in love.

J.E.M.

56

Here's another possibility:

Leader: We gather together today because we feel called to do so.
People: We gather because we have people in our lives we want to remember.
Leader: These are people who have meant the world to us, even people who have *given* the world to us, and now our world seems emptier without them.
People: We gather because there have been events in our lives which have shaped who we are today.
Leader: We have been changed by what has happened to us, and we are changing still, as we adapt in the ways we must, as we grow in the ways we're led.
People: We gather because we dare not forget.
Leader: We dare not forget that we have known joy in its many forms and contentment with its many faces. We dare not forget that we have been enriched in many, many ways.
People: We gather because we want to give evidence of our love.
Leader: We come together today to affirm that we have loved, that we have *been* loved, and that we love and are being loved still.
People: We gather together today to assert our belief: true love never dies. And for that we will always be thankful.

J.E.M.

A number of psalms can serve to direct people's thoughts. Try one of these: Psalm 27, Psalm 90, Psalm 121, or Psalm 139. They can be used in whole or in part, either spoken by a leader, read in unison, or recited responsively. Spend some time looking through the words of hymns and songs; sometimes these words read aloud contain a message that's not always heard when they're sung.

Try writing your own words for your group to read. If you do so, create breaks in your sentences so people know where to pause in their reading. Use repetitive phrases sometimes. Keep your language direct and simple. Make sure your words are inclusive in every sense. And avoid having people say what may not ring true for them. Go for the universal; it's often the more personal.

Some other possibilities are these:

For everything there is a season and a time for every matter under heaven:
a time to be born, and a time to die;
a time to plant, and a time to pluck up what is planted;
a time to kill, and a time to heal;
a time to break down, and a time to build up;
a time to weep, and a time to laugh;
a time to mourn, and a time to dance;
a time to cast away stones, and a time to gather stones to-gether;
a time to embrace, and a time to refrain from embracing;
a time to seek, and a time to lose;
a time to keep, and a time to cast away;
a time to rend, and a time to sew;
a time to keep silence, and a time to speak;
a time to love, and a time to hate;
a time for war, and a time for peace.
Ecclesiastes 3

We give back to You, O God, those whom You gave us. You did not lose them when You gave them to us, and we do not lose them by their return to You. We have been taught that life is eternal and love cannot die. So death is only a horizon, and a horizon is only the limit of our sight. Open our eyes to see more clearly, and draw us closer to You, that we may know we are nearer to our loved ones, who are with You.
William Penn (adapted)

Lord our God, from whom neither life nor death can separate those who trust in Your love, and whose love holds in its embrace Your children in this world and the next; so unite us to Yourself that in fellowship with You we may always be united to our loved ones whether here or there. Give us courage, constancy, and hope.

William Temple (adapted)

Lord, teach me the silence of love, the silence of wisdom, the silence of humility, the silence of faith, the silence that speaks without words. Teach me to silence my heart that I may listen to the gentle movement of the Spirit within me, and sense the depths which are God, today and always.

Sixteenth century prayer

Remember me when I am gone away,
Gone far away into the silent land;
When you can no more hold me by the hand,
Nor I half turn to go, yet turning stay.
Remember me when no more, day by day,
You tell me of our future that you planned:
Only remember me; you understand
It will be late to counsel then or pray.
Yet if you should forget me for a while
And afterwards remember, do not grieve:
For if the darkness and corruption leave
A vestige of the thoughts that once I had,
Better by far you should forget and smile
Than that you should remember and be sad.

Christina Rossetti

Something has spoken to me in the night,
Burning the tapers of the waning years;
Something has spoken in the night,
And told me I shall die, I know not where.
Saying:
"To lose the earth you know, for greater knowing;
To lose the life you have, for greater life;
To leave the friends you loved, for greater loving;
To find a land more kind than home, more large than earth."

Thomas Wolfe

You left, but you left peace of your own gifting,
Imparted gently through the quiet years;
You left, but you left goodness so uplifting
That each remembering only endears.

You left, but your soft steps of sympathy
Move still to each soul turbulent in need,
Your gentle going did not set you free
Of hearts who loved you through each selfless deed.

Your ministering spirit warms us still.
Your seeds of goodness still continue growing,
You left so much of love it seems to fill
The very emptiness about your going.
Your presence was a blessing so very dear
That even in your absence you are near.

Betty W. Stoffel

Death is nothing at all; it does not count. I have only
slipped away into the next room. Nothing has happened;
everything remains exactly as it was. I am I, and you are you,
and the old life that we lived so fondly together is untouched,
unchanged. What we were to each other, we are still. Call
me by the old familiar name. Speak to me in that easy way
you always used. Put no difference in your tone. Wear no
false air of solemnity or sorrow. Laugh as we always laughed
at the little jokes that we enjoyed together. Play, smile, think
of me, pray for me. Let my name be ever the household
word that it always was. Let it be spoken without effort,
without the ghost of a shadow upon it. Life means all that it
has ever meant. It is the same as it always was. There is
absolute and unbroken continuity. What is this death, but
negligible accident? I am but waiting for you, for an interval
somewhere, very near, just around the corner. All is well.
Nothing is past; nothing is lost. One brief moment, and all
will be as it was before.

Canon Henry Scott-Holland

Welcome, Lord, into your calm and peaceful kingdom those who, out of this present life, have departed to be with you; grant them rest and a place with the spirits of the just; and give them the life that knows not age, the reward that passes not away.

Ignatius Loyola

This part of your service might contain a prayer, not just for those who have died, but for those who remember and long for those who have died. It might include a time of silent meditation, allowing memories to form their own sort of prayer.

This is also a good time to include one or two songs or hymns, if that seems appropriate for your gathering. A good song leader is critically important for a group of people who have not sung together before, especially if they do not know the music well. An alternative might be one or more songs by a singer or a chorus, perhaps including a refrain on which people could join in. Choose music that carries a message of hope.

The Third Part: A Time of Reflecting

The people who have accepted your invitation to participate in this special time will appreciate your having prepared for them in an additional way. They will hunger for a message that addresses what's presently happening to them on the level of their heart and soul. These are the kinds of questions they may carry within:

• Why did this death occur? Why did it occur at this time? Why does death happen at all?

• Why am I grieving so? Will this grief ever end?

• Why does it hurt so to remember? Should I keep remembering? Or should I try to forget?

• What has happened to the one I love? Will we meet

again? Are they okay? How can I know that?

• What if I've lost my reason to live? What does that mean?

• Will I ever get over this? Can I ever be happy again? *Should* I be happy again?

• Is it possible that the one who died can still be a part of my life? If so, how? How can I know?

• What is there to hope for from here? What can be the sources of my hope?

You need not—indeed, you cannot—answer all these questions. You haven't the time and your audience hasn't the energy. Some questions may not be answerable. But those who have accepted your invitation deserve to be given something that confirms them and gives them hope.

One solution is to ask a person to address your group for a few moments—five or ten minutes maybe, no more than fifteen. A clergyperson is one choice, and often a good one; she or he will have had experience performing similar functions in the past. But keep your options open before you decide. Is there a community elder your audience respects? An author or a poet? A professor? Someone who's a living example of how grief has taken them to another level in their life?

The purpose of this message is not so much education as it is inspiration, not fact but hope. A meditation can do that. So can a meaningful story or a thoughtful reading. So can an audiovisual presentation.

The video *We Will Remember: A Meditation for Those Who Live On* was first created as the centerpiece for a time of reflecting at a service of remembrance. A transcript of its narration can be found in the appendix. There are other audiovisual presentations that can work as well. Your group might even want to create its own.

If you use a videotape, make sure that everyone will be able to see the screen with ease. A single TV monitor will probably work for 40 or 50 people. Two regular monitors or a large-screen monitor or a video projector may be needed for larger groups.

Should you elect to use the *We Will Remember* video, either as a message by itself or following a spoken meditation, you might use this responsive reading afterward:

Leader: Let us make our remembering more than a remembering. Let us make it a hope and a pledge, carried on these words:
People: In the summer sun and fields of brightness, we will remember. In the autumn haze and blazes of color, we will remember. In the winter chill and blankets of whiteness, we will remember. And in the warmth of spring and bursts of new life, we will remember.
Leader: With everything that is permanent, and with all that is passing,
People: With everything that is majestic and with all that is common,
Leader: With everything that carries us in concern and with all that lifts us in joy,
People: We will remember again and again and again.
Leader: As long as we have life, we will remember.
People: And in the remembering we will discover new life, new hope, and new courage, and if not today, then tomorrow.
J.E.M.

The Fourth Part: A Time of Remembering

This part of your service has the potential for being especially meaningful to your participants. This will be an opportunity for them to symbolically and publicly recognize the life of the one they miss. They'll receive a permission from you that they'll probably not receive from many other people in their lives, and they'll be grateful. They'll be able to truly mourn their loss.

One of the magic elements of ritual is that it gives people a contained space in which they can address the enormity of what has happened to them. Sometimes people are afraid to give way to their feelings, wondering if they will be able to stop crying once they start. By creating a beginning, a middle, and an end to this ceremony, you set limits on this time and give your participants a sense of safety. By the design of your event you communicate, "First we'll ease into our feelings, then we'll feel them, then we'll release them, then we'll gradually return to the way we began. Only we won't end up exactly where we were when we started—we will have moved forward a bit."

As you consider the type of commemoration that will be a centering piece for your event, keep these suggestions in mind:

• *Keep your commemoration simple.* Develop one main idea, then let other plans flow from that one. Attempting to carry out or unite two or three different ideas will confuse people and dilute the impact of a single, meaningful act. Remember that people in grief often have shortened attention spans and may have difficulty following complex directions. They have plenty on their minds already.

• *Allow for the expression of feelings.* That's what many people need. That's one way their grief naturally emerges. But don't program particular kinds of feelings and certainly don't encourage pure sentimentalism. Design a thoughtful, quiet, dignified ceremony and let people bring whatever feelings they have and leave with whatever insights and assurances they will. Some people may bring no feelings, or at least it may seem so. They deserve validation too.

• *Consider designing the commemoration so that participants can take a symbol of the ceremony with them.* This might be a candle they may burn again at home, or a holiday ornament they may place somewhere special, or a memento they can carry in their pocket or purse. It's another way to remember their loved one and a way to carry the learnings and meanings of this day through the days ahead.

• *Encourage the participation of everyone.* That includes people of all ages, all abilities, all situations. If children are in attendance, make it as natural for them to take part as anyone else. Make sure someone who understands children's needs and thoughts helps design your ceremony.

• *Include everyone, but don't mandate participation.* For all sorts of reasons, some may wish to sit and watch. Help them feel comfortable with that decision.

One of the more popular commemorations is a candlelighting ceremony. Its effect is visually beautiful and it's also physically calming. It contains both a private dimension (lighting one's own candle while holding the thought of a loved one very close) and a public dimension (sharing the light with one another and basking in the common light provided by all the candles). This is often a very moving ceremony.

The following litany might be used:

Leader: A century and a half ago Henry Ward Beecher spoke for all of us when he said, "What the heart has once owned and had, it shall never lose." Today we pay homage to those whom our hearts have owned and had, and whom we know we shall never lose.
People: We recall those who have been the very life of life to us, those whom we shall never forget.
Leader: We come together today to remember those who have touched our lives in such a way that we will never be the same. We are changed by having known them.
People: We shall always be indebted for what they have given us, and thankful for what they have shown us, and grateful for the ways in which they have blessed our lives.
Leader: Let us remember those who have been as light of light to us, memorializing our relationships in this ceremony of candlelight and love.

*First Candlelighter:*We light a candle in memory of those who have handed us the gift of life itself. We honor those who gave us birth and nurtured us, those who endowed us with heritage and raised us, those who offered us love and cherished us.

People: We remember mothers and fathers, grandparents and great-grandparents, and all our ancestors through the ages. We remember also those who were as mother or father to us, loving us by choice rather than by chance.

Second Candlelighter: We light a candle in memory of those who have been linked with us in the ongoing chain of family life. We honor those who have shared our heredity and who have experienced our common bonds.

People: We remember sisters and brothers, aunts and uncles, relatives near and distant throughout time.

Third Candlelighter: We light a candle in memory of those to whom we ourselves have passed on the precious gift of life. We hold dear to our hearts those we have held dear in our arms and in our dreams.

People: We remember children who have gone before us, and grandchildren, and great-grandchildren. We remember both those who lived within the womb and those who danced upon the earth.

Fourth Candlelighter: We light a candle in memory of those whom we discovered through the eyes of love in our journey through life. We hold sacred the remembrances of those who brightened our days with affection and who lit up our lives with devotion.

People: We remember wives and husbands, dearest lovers and closest friends, those who opened us to ourselves and to life even as we opened ourselves to them and now to eternity.

Fifth Candlelighter: We light a candle in memory of those who have walked beside us in so many ways. We remember ones who worked with us and played with us, ones who have made our time on earth more enjoyable and our experiences in this world more memorable.

People: We remember friends and associates, those who

66

neighbored us and lifted us and expanded our horizons.
Leader: We leave the final candle unlit, aware of the fact that others will join our ranks in days to come, that they are doing so even now. They will stand where we now stand, and feel what we now feel. Our hearts reach out to them.
People: We remember also that the time will come when we ourselves will pass through the barrier separating one form of life from another. We know that as we remember today, we will be remembered tomorrow.

J.E.M.

This litany calls for the lighting of several commemorative candles in front of the entire gathering. If you adopt or adapt this procedure, make sure the candles are large enough to be seen by everyone, and placed in a prominent position. Select candles that allow the flame to be clearly visible from a seated position. You might place the candles in a candelabra, or on an altar-like table with each candle having its own stand.

Light each of the candles slowly and ceremonially at the appropriate time. Rather than matches, use a long taper or something similar, taking the light from a flame that has been burning throughout the service.

Consider involving all participants who so desire in the act of candlelighting. People might be given their own small tapers to carry, lighting them from their choice of the five large ones as they walk by. Or the light might be passed from the front of the room, aisle by aisle, person to person, until the entire room is aglow. In some situations participants might stand in a circle, watching as the flame fans from the center outward, or around the circumference.

Make sure that people know to light their candles by holding the candle to be lit at an angle, moving it toward the burning candle which is held stationary and upright. Use protectors on each candle to keep the wax from dripping.

Allow the candles to burn for awhile so that people may savor the experience. They will not want to rush. Arrange for a song to be sung, a piece of music to be performed or played, or prepared words to be spoken. Silence can also be very effective. If your group is smaller, people's thoughts or memories might be shared informally.

Extinguishing the candles may be an emotional time for those who have identified with this experience. Help make it easier for people to blow out their flame by reminding participants that the light of their memories and the influence of the other's life are not being extinguished. They will burn on as before, deep within and even all around.

Your group might use votive candles rather than tapers. These may be held by individuals or placed in a certain location before the group. Sometimes they are placed to form a familiar shape—a heart, a tree, a circle, a star, or perhaps some symbol that has been used earlier in your ceremony. Some groups send floating candles onto a pool or pond.

People often like to take their candles home, both as a reminder of the event and for use in their own private ritual afterward. For that reason you might wish to purchase candles large enough to be used more than once.

Another way to ritualize the memories of loved ones is to create a large banner upon which pictures, photographs, and personal messages can be placed. Individuals and families might write letters, poems, and affirmations, affix them to a piece of felt already cut in the shape of a heart or circle or square, and then attach this to a large hanging banner with pins or Velcro. More complex creations might be sewn together like a quilt. Banners might be built, adding square upon square, memory upon memory. Once completed, these creations can be dedicated in a simple act and perhaps later placed in a public location for others to view.

Some groups find meaning in decorating a holiday tree. Ornaments can be created using names, words, pictures, and photographs and then placed on the branches. Such a tree might be ceremonially lit. Another option is to decorate such a tree with ornaments which look alike except that each is marked with the name of one who has died.

Memory books can be created and displayed. Slide shows or videotapes can be produced and shared. Trees can be planted. Flowers may be given away. Memories can be written as stories and read aloud, or as letters and placed in a specially-decorated box for safekeeping. A popular ceremony has been to release helium-filled balloons, sometimes with messages attached. Be aware there has been concern about the ecological wisdom of this practice.

Adapt ceremonies that arise from your faith practices. Learn from some of the newer funeral liturgies. Find ways that allow people to say and do publicly what they wish they had been encouraged to share in the past.

To repeat: remain sensitive to the fact that people will bring plenty of their own emotions to this event. Provide quiet outlets and natural ways for them to explore their thoughts and feelings. Don't program them, but allow them to do what they need.

The Fifth Part: A Time of Integrating

Once your ceremony has interwoven its main elements and people have performed their rituals of remembrance, the next movement is to prepare participants to return from this experience. It's a time to integrate what has occurred so it can be internalized and taken with them.

It's already been noted that people need verbal assurance and gentle encouragement if there's been a candlelighting ceremony and people's candles are to be extinguished before people leave. Instructing people how to visualize moving the flame inside themselves is one way to help make this transition. Another way is to remind them they can recreate a similar ritual on their own. People deserve thoughtful assistance, whatever the nature of their ritual, if this time has touched them at a deep level. This should be done sensitively and confidently, in an unhurried manner.

Someone who has led an earlier part of your ritual might speak a few words, summarizing what has occurred and emphasizing the healing quality of what has begun. Sometimes it helps for people to know that they may feel a little more tearful or a little sadder for a short time—that can be the very sign, in fact, that healing energy is at work. People may be encouraged to seek out someone with whom they can talk.

Perhaps a song can be sung or performed, one that will move people's thoughts in the direction of returning to their everyday life a little more enriched for what they've experienced. Moments of blessing can occur when people hold hands or link arms, expressing the closeness they feel and demonstrating the commonality they share. As always, people deserve permission not to touch or be touched in this way if they so choose.

A statement of belief might have a place. For example:

There is no denying it: it hurts to lose.
It hurts to lose a cherished relationship with one we love.
It hurts to lose that which has united us with the past,
     or that which has beckoned us into the future.
Yet we affirm there is more to losing than just hurt and pain,
     for there are other experiences loss calls forth as well.
We believe courage can also appear:
     the courage to be strong enough to surrender,
          the fortitude to be firm enough to be flexible,
               the bravery to go where one has not gone before.

We believe a time of loss can be a time of learning
   unlike any other,
     and that it can teach some of life's most valuable lessons:
In the act of losing, there is something to be found.
In the act of letting go, there is something to be grasped.
In the act of saying "goodbye," there is a "hello" to be heard.
For living with loss is about endings as well as beginnings.
And grieving is a matter of life as much as death.
And loving is a matter of eternity more than of time.
So it has always been, and so it shall always be.
                J.E.M.

The Sixth Part: A Time of Departing

The final act is to put an ending to your commemoration and to signal people's options as they prepare to leave. A song of departure might be sung or played, a prayer read together, or a benediction spoken—or all of the above. Possibilities include:

If you would indeed behold the spirit of death,
   open your heart wide unto the body of life.
For life and death are one,
   even as the river and the sea are one.
          Kahlil Gibran

She whom we love and lose is no longer where she was before. She is now wherever we are.
          John Chrysostom

They are alive and well somewhere,
The smallest sprout shows there is really no death,
And if there ever was, it led forward life,
and does not wait at the end to arrest it,
And ceas'd the moment life appear'd.
          Walt Whitman

When I die if you need to weep
Cry for your brother or sister
Walking the street beside you
And when you need me put your arms around anyone
And give them what you need to give me.

I want to leave you something
Something better than words or sounds.

Look for me in the people I've known or loved
And if you cannot give me away
At least let me live in your eyes and not on your mind.

You can love me most by letting hands touch hands
By letting bodies touch bodies
And by letting go of children that need to be free.

Love doesn't die, people do
So when all that's left of me is love
Give me away.

Author unknown

Inside this new love, die.
Your way begins on the other side.
Become the sky.
Take an axe to the prison wall.
Escape.
Walk out like someone suddenly born into color.
Do it now.

Rumi

Lord, the day is yours, and the night is yours; you have prepared the light and the sun; they continue this day according to your ordinance, for all things serve you. Blessed are you, O Lord, for you turn the shadow of death into the morning.

Lancelot Andrewes

In the shade I will believe
what in the sun I loved.
                        Henry David Thoreau

I shall remember while the light lives yet
And in the night time I shall not forget.
                        Algernon Charles Swinburne

Leader: There is an old proverb: "Good ones must die, but death cannot kill their names." We know that yesterday's wisdom carries still today's truth.
People: We know that good ones must die, but we refuse to believe that is the final word.
Leader: Someone who has shared time on earth beside us has died,
People: But death cannot kill their name.
Leader: Someone we have grown to love has gone on without us,
People: But death cannot kill their name.
Leader: Someone who was close to us is no longer close in the same way,
People: But death cannot kill their name.
Leader: We know that these we cherish have left indelible marks on our lives,
People: And therefore we know that death cannot kill their name.
Leader: They have etched their faces on our souls,
People: And therefore we affirm that death cannot kill their name.
Leader: They are now a part of us and a part of all life in a way they have never been.
People: So we assert, both now and forever, that no matter what happens, death cannot kill their name. It will live on in us, and through us, and far beyond us.
                        J.E.M.

73

Lord, make me an instrument of your peace.
Where there is hatred, let me sow love;
Where there is injury, pardon;
Where there is doubt, faith;
Where there is despair, hope;
Where there is darkness, light;
Where is sadness, joy.
O divine Master, grant that I may not so much seek
To be consoled, as to console,
To be understood, as to understand,
To be loved, as to love,
For it is in giving that we receive;
It is in pardoning that we are pardoned;
It is in dying that we are born to eternal life.

Francis of Assissi

Do not stand at my grave and weep;
I am not there. I do not sleep.
I am a thousand winds that blow.
I am the diamond glints on snow.
I am the sunlight on ripened grain.
I am the gentle autumn's rain.
When you awaken in the morning's hush,
I am the swift uplifting rush
Of quiet birds in circled flight.
I am the soft stars that shine at night.
Do not stand at my grave and cry.
I am not there. I did not die.

Clare Harner Lyon

Yet Love will dream and Faith will trust
Since He who knows our need is just,
That somewhere, somehow, meet we must.
Alas for him who never sees
The stars shine through his cypress-trees;
Who hopeless lays his dead away,

Nor look to see the breaking day
Across the mournful marbles play;
Who hath not learned, in hours of faith,
The truth to flesh and sense unknown,
That life is ever Lord of death,
And love can never lose its own!

John Greenleaf Whittier

The Lord watch between me and thee
    while we are absent one from another.

Genesis 31

What the heart has once owned and had,
    it shall never lose.

Henry Ward Beecher

Teach me the power and the strength of silence, that I
may go into the world as still as a mouse in the depths of my
heart.

Mechtild of Madgeburg

Be thou a bright flame before me,
Be thou a guiding star above me,
Be thou a smooth path below me,
Be thou a kindly shepherd behind me,
Today, tonight, and forever.

St. Columba

May the road rise up to meet you,
may the wind be always at your back,
may the sun shine upon your face,
the rains fall soft upon your field
and, until we meet again,
may God hold you in the palm of God's hand.

Ancient Irish blessing

One more suggestion: if you give out a printed program for your service, consider making it of "collector quality." This might mean having it professionally typeset or composed on a laser printer, perhaps even designed by a graphic artist. Try using more than one color of ink, or an ink color other than black. Select paper stock that communicates "permanence" or "importance." Your attendees may wish to share this program with others, or they may want to read it over themselves, or they may choose to preserve it as a keepsake. In this way, as in other ways, the good you are doing will last longer than you might expect.

7

Getting Out the Word

The success of your holiday event will depend upon one factor as much as any other: how much people are aware of what you're going to do and when and where you'll do it. If you design a wonderful program and hardly anyone is there to participate because they didn't hear about it, the results will be less than wonderful.

Getting out the word is not just an "add-on," something you do just before your event occurs and everything is finally in place. The marketing should begin as soon as the decision has been made to sponsor this event and your basic plans are in place. It will work best if there is one member of your steering committee or one sub-group who will oversee this task, but that doesn't mean one person or one small group must do all the work. It means they will *coordinate* the work. The entire planning committee should remain in involved with the marketing, if only slightly.

You dare not rely upon only one method to publicize your event. The more people you plan to inform, the more means you'll need to use and the more often you'll need to use them. If yours is a closed invitation (inviting only the members of one organization, for example), you may get by with using only a couple or three methods. If you want to make anyone in your larger community feel welcome, you will need to plan many more thrusts—maybe ten or twenty different ones.

You don't have to spend a lot of money to do this. More than anything else, your task requires ingenuity and persistence. Moreover, you probably *shouldn't* spend a lot of money. It can be a mistake if your program appears too "slick." The people you want to attract will resist a Madison

Avenue approach. They won't want pizzazz—they'll want to feel someone within their community has taken the time to provide honest, thoughtful, caring assistance for people like themselves. That's something money doesn't buy.

Marketing to a Closed Group

If your plan is to appeal only to a group in which most people already know one another or where there's already regular communication among members, your job is comparatively easy. You can use the means at hand to inform and to invite.

If you're preparing a program for a congregation, for example, you'll use the systems that are already in place: the congregational newsletter, the worship bulletin, announcements at meetings, signs on bulletin boards, perhaps a short, live presentation before your group. Begin early, make your message clear and consistent, and explain to people what they're to do if they want to attend. Presuming there's truly a need for a program of this sort, and there's no schedule conflicts, and yours is a healthy organization, you'll be on your way.

Marketing to the Community at Large

Your work is cut out for you if you wish to draw people you don't know, and people who don't know you, especially if they've never heard of a program like this before. It will take time to lay the groundwork. It will mean paying attention to details so that nothing is overlooked. A certain amount of hard work is unavoidable. Your efforts will especially benefit from a splash—or better yet, a bucketload—of creative thinking.

As you ponder how you'll get the word out, keep these four principles in mind:

- *The media need you in the same way you need them.*

Some people feel they should approach newspaper reporters and radio and TV personalities on bended knee. That's not necessary. Yes, you'll need what they have to offer—a way to get your message before large numbers of people. But remember they also need people like you and events like yours if they're to give their subscribers something to read about and their listeners and viewers something interesting to hear and to see. In fact, yours is the kind of story that may catch their fancy. It's unusual. It's an obvious benefit to many. It's the kind of story news media often enjoy giving special attention.

Approach the media cordially, confidently, and professionally. Share what you have to offer, knowing it will help you, but also knowing it will assist them to meet their own goals. Make it easy for them to do their job. Provide information in the form they request. Avoid wordiness. Meet their deadlines. Be available. Be accurate. Follow through. But you don't have to kowtow to them. Make them a part of your team and become a solid member of theirs.

- *People don't always see well or listen right and they can have terrible memories.*

Most everyone is bombarded every day with messages of every sort. From the time we awaken in the morning until we drift off to sleep at night, someone is vying for our attention, wanting us to try something, buy something, experience something, or believe something. They use every available means to get us to concentrate on what they want us to—billboards, computer screens, magazine pages, newspaper headlines, streamers behind airplanes, on and on. Obviously, you have some competition out there.

Remember that people may not remember your message until they've been exposed to it a number of times. They may not be ready to do anything until they've been reminded again and again. And even then, they may wait until the last minute. So get your message out in as many ways as possible. Repeat yourself. Try little variations in what you say or write, maintaining your basic message throughout. Keep doing this until you're sure you've done it too much. That will mean you've done it almost enough.

• *Nothing has yet replaced the power of word-of-mouth.*

People believe people they know. They believe what is said when there are no underlying motives at play. So talk about what you're planning. Share it with your family, your friends, your colleagues, your neighbors. Share it with perfect strangers. Chat about it at work, at parties, on the golf course, at the store. Encourage others to talk about it too. Save your breath and use computer email. Then turn around and save your fingers by using the telephone.

• *If you don't know where you're going, you probably won't get there.*

If you don't know which people you want to communicate with, you won't find them. If you don't have a plan for how you'll do what you need to do, you won't do it, or at least you won't do it very well. You'll fudge. You'll drift.

Identify your intended audience. Who are they? Where are they? How can they be reached? Who and what can help you reach them? What's the first thing you'll need to do? The sixth? The twenty-sixth? When should each of those things be done? By whom? For how long?

Write your plan. Be specific about tasks, dates, people and places. Keep notes on everything you do. Next year you'll be glad you did.

A Flyer

A colorful flyer or brochure will perhaps be a mainstay for your marketing. You can mail these pieces, hand them out, and leave them for people to pick up. They can be produced comparatively inexpensively. In fact, they may even be free for you. A printing company might donate them to your cause. The printing department or the marketing arm of a large local business might do the same. Even if such donations are not options, you can still have something printed for pennies per piece.

Don't get fancy. Use standard size paper, either 8½ by 11 or 8½ by 14. Design it so it folds to fit into a regular envelope and so it's easy to carry. Make one panel a cover and another panel the place for an address label. Check with your post office about any technicalities: mailing permits, sealing tabs, return addresses, and so on.

Keep your flyer simple, clean, and clear. Use just one or two typestyles. Don't crowd your design. Make everything easy enough for a ninth grader to read. Write in short sentences. Use active verbs. Spice it up if you want with some little graphic elements or maybe a photograph or two. Perhaps a graphic artist will volunteer to help you. But you can also get amazing results on your own with some of the newer computer software programs.

Include a telephone number people can call with their questions. If you encourage pre-registration, include a sign-up form within your flyer. An email address might help.

Print more of these flyers than you think you'll need. You'll use them.

News Releases

A news release gives you credibility. It tells the media that you know about marketing and public relations. They know they can count on you to be reliable and professional.

Most news releases follow a standard format. Put "for immediate release" at the top of your page. Write about your event as if you were writing a newspaper article. Put the basic information (who, what, when, where, why) in the first paragraph. Add other interesting facts in succeeding paragraphs, from most to least important. Place the name, address, and daytime and evening telephone numbers of your contact person at the bottom, right after the words "for more information contact." Put all this on one side of one page if possible, but never use more than two pages. Use your group's letterhead if you wish, or just use plain paper.

Mail it to the various news media, including a short cover letter introducing your group and your event. Send out this release six to eight weeks before your program. Write another one a couple weeks before your event, emphasizing a different angle: something about your keynote speaker perhaps, or what's noteworthy about your ritual of commemoration. Fax this one. Fax another one early in the morning the day before your event if you're hoping for on-site coverage of your proceedings.

Newspapers

In addition to sending a press release, contact a reporter from your area newspaper or newspapers. If you don't know one by name, ask for a feature reporter or the feature editor. Explain what you're planning and ask if a special article might be printed a week or so before your event. Volunteer to provide background information about grief and the holidays. Give them the name of a professional or two they might interview by telephone. Or maybe they'll want to talk with a grieving person who'll be attending your event.

Compile whatever information they request, then let them determine the scope of their article. They'll have a clear idea what they consider newsworthy. Perhaps they'll do two side-by-side articles—one about the nature of grief or the problem of holiday grief and another about your event.

Depending upon your newspaper's policy and your community's size, an article may or may not run after your event. One way you can keep your program in front of people is to write a letter to the editor afterwards, thanking all the volunteers and participants and adding some positive comments about the day itself. Letters to the editor are among the most popular parts of most newspapers.

If you have a budget, you can always pay for newspaper advertising. Notices in the public announcements section in the classified ads usually aren't very costly. A small display ad near the funeral notices might catch the eye of those who would be interested.

Radio and Television

Try to get on as many programs as you can a week or two before your event. Just because one station carries your story doesn't mean another cannot or will not. Ask about talk shows and interview programs. Some stations will carry something short in a news program right after your event, especially if there's something unusual about it: a lot of people came, or something colorful happened, or this was the "first ever" event.

Certain stations will even create a PSA or public service announcement for you and air it from time to time at no cost to you. FCC regulations require them to demonstrate their commitment to community service. Can you think of any better way for them to do that? It's possible they may choose to run these "spots" at those times when they're short on regular paid advertising.

Put your best foot forward in these media appearances. Arrange for people to represent you who can speak concisely and eloquently and who think well on their feet.

If a station has worked extra hard to present your story, send them an appreciative letter. Address it to the general manager and send a copy to the reporter or camera person who did so much.

Don't forget cable TV stations. Use their community bulletin boards. Arrange to host a call-in program before your event. Videotape a part of your proceedings and then broadcast it as a cable TV program afterward. Just make sure you protect the privacy of of your attendees.

Other Opportunities

You'll want to check into all those opportunities that are unique to your community. Each area has its own traditions and possibilities.

• *Billboards.* Some billboard companies will supply space for community service programs, just as other media do. Otherwise you'll have to buy it. A billboard official can explain how to design these special ads so they communicate quickly and easily.

• *Speakers bureau.* Create a speakers bureau just for your event. Publicize that you have people who can give short talks and presentations about grief and the holidays. Send letters to all the organizations and associations you can think of, especially those which have regular meetings and are always looking for speakers.

• *Private newsletters.* Hospitals often publish their own newsletters, both for their in-house staff and for the larger community. Your program is in keeping with their overall goal of health promotion. You could be seen as an extension of their chaplaincy program or their social service staff. Medium- and large-size corporations often have similar publications and they're usually looking for programs that support the emotional well-being of their employees.

• *Public newsletters and mailings.* Public utilities and local telephone companies often include an informative mailing with their monthly bills. Sometimes local or area governmental agencies publish informative mailings. Look around.

• *Congregations.* Churches and synagogues are good

prospects to help spread the word, since your program will help their people. Check into clergy organizations too.

• *Funeral homes.* If anyone understands the importance of what you're doing, it ought to be these professionals. Will they display stacks of your flyers? Include one in each packet that goes to a bereaved family? Allow you to use their mailing list of clients?

• *Hospices.* Hospices are mandated to serve bereaved families for thirteen months following the death of a hospice patient. It's hard to find a more knowledgeable, dedicated group of people who are sensitive to the needs of those who are grieving.

• *Obstetricians and hospital childbirth professionals.* These are the people most aware of neonatal losses and stillbirths. They're often anxious to offer help and yet they realize their own helplessness. You have a partial solution for them.

• *Oncologists and hospital oncology professionals.* These people know about another sort of death. They also get to know surviving family members and become aware of their needs.

• *Grief-related support groups.* Those informal networks of suicide survivors, grieving parents, grieving siblings, grieving spouses, and others are exactly where your materials can do the most good.

• *Elder adult programs.*

• *Mental health professionals in private practice.*

• *Hospital chaplains and social workers.*

• *Employee assistance programs in corporations.*

• *School counselors.*

Your community will have its own networks. Some grocery store chains will print a public service announcement on their paper bags or place your flyer with each customer's order. Some corporations will include a short notice inside the envelopes containing employees' paychecks. Think about the civic-minded businesses in your area. How might they support you? Would an advertising agency lend you their expertise?

Schedule a creative thinking session with your steering committee or with another group of individuals. Start with this ground rule: there's no such thing as a bad idea. Draw up a list of all sorts of possibilities for spreading the word. Build on one another's ideas. Get zany. Then go back and sort out those ideas that might work in your situation. You may use only a handful from the long list you developed, but that handful will be golden.

Give the marketing of your event the attention it deserves. Do it for those who will benefit the most: those who are grieving and grasping for help.

8

Concluding Thoughts

Let's say you've planned your event carefully and thoughtfully. You've gathered a group of people who functioned well together as leaders, facilitators, coordinators, and helpers. You've done your marketing conscientiously and consistently. You've arranged for the efficient use of your facilities and your event has unfolded smoothly and fairly predictably. From what you can tell, your participants are glad they attended and there is a sense of satisfaction in the air as you time together ends. You're glad your work is now done.

Be aware: your work is not yet done. Your event is not over just because your program indicates it is.

It's already been noted that the day's discussions and activities may activate or re-activate certain feelings in some participants. That may or may not come as a surprise to them. Should such feelings occur, these people may have someone to support them as they leave or once they return home. Then again, they may not.

It will be important to be sensitive to how people are responding throughout your event and especially as your event ends. While it's not necessarily common, sometimes you may find a person who's crying hard or showing other signs of distress. This can also happen to a whole family. It will be wise if you have one or more professionals on hand monitoring what's happening as people are about to leave, so they can spend time with these people if it seems appropriate.

Some people may wish to remain seated for awhile, even a long while, if this experience has touched them or if they have felt a special connection with the one who has died.

They deserve their quietness and they should not be rushed. Perhaps others will wish to speak to someone about what this event has meant to them or what it has raised within them. It will help if you can provide a quiet, private space or two where they can talk with a trained counselor or with one of the day's leaders. These conversations need not be lengthy.

It may be appropriate to refer a person to a grief counselor or another professional for follow-up work. Give people a choice of names, if you can, rather than a single name. Another option is to inform people about any grief support groups in your community. Have names, telephone numbers, meeting times and locations available as handouts. Depending upon the circumstances, you may wish to call a person who's been distraught later in the evening or the next day, letting them know they're not alone.

Another concluding exercise will be the evaluation of your event. Perhaps you'll encourage your participants to use an evaluation form you've created and made available to them. Begin by listing the various parts of your event with a place to rate each one, maybe on a scale from 1 to 5, from "less helpful" to "more helpful" or "less meaningful" to "very meaningful." Have a place for them to write their general comments too. Make sure they have plenty of room to write. Ask for their suggestions for the future. If you make this form easy to use, more people will use it, giving you a more accurate and detailed overall response. Don't just read these forms; tabulate them and then analyze your tabulations.

Schedule a final meeting with your steering committee and continue the evaluation process. Talk with one another about your event. What worked especially well? What worked less well? What was missing from your event? What surprised you? What would it help for you to do next time? Look into all the aspects of your event, including your schedule, location, and publicity. Study the participants' evaluations and add to your knowledge. Is there consensus about any changes that are called for? What are they? Be specific. Keep a record of all your thoughts.

This is a good time to decide about next steps. Did this event fill a definite need? Should there be another event like this one? If there *should* be, then *will* there be? Who'll do what to organize it? When will that begin? If you decide to proceed, try to set the date as quickly as possible, even if you do nothing more at this point.

What else did you learn about grieving people and their needs? Is your organization or your community doing what's important for them? Is there more to be done? Brainstorm about the possibilities. What might happen between now and a year from now? What groups might be organized? What others sorts of events might be sponsored? What training is called for? You may or may not have the re-sources to do any of these extra things, but at least you'll have taken your task seriously. Maybe you'll be more prepared to do something in a year or two.

Show appreciation to the people who made this event possible. Make sure your steering committee feels good about what they've done. Send notes and letters to people who donated anything, whether it was themselves or something that belonged to them.

I hope you'll discover what so many others have discov-ered: helping bereaved people prepare for the holiday period is more a worthy endeavor—it's a life-affirming experience that directly affects how people heal as they grieve. You'll help people mourn what they deserve to mourn so that one day their sense of liveliness will return. You'll validate people's losses and in the process you'll start a chain reaction. These people will learn to validate these losses themselves, and other losses in the future. They'll learn to appreciate and normalize the losses of other people around them. Then dying and death, loss and grief won't be hidden from view so easily. It will be what it should be, what it already is: a natural, healthy part of life.

Mostly I hope you'll learn this secret: no one will benefit from what you do any more than you.

Appendix

Following is a transcript of the Willowgreen videotape,
We Will Remember: A Meditation for Those Who Live On,
which was originally created for rituals of remembrance.
This video incorporates photography from nature and
original music with the narration.

There are times in our lives when we remember.
Life was unfolding before us, unfolding within us.
There was an uncurling, an opening up.
We were seeking the light,
    and, just as much, the light was seeking us.
There was so much to see, to feel.
Rich textures, vivid colors, bold tapestries.
This was not a perfect time.
Long spells on this earth seldom are.
Were it in our power, we would make changes.
But there was so much that was good.
So many possibilities before us.
So many reasons to be thankful.
Tenderness we knew, and closeness.
And the comfort of knowing that where we were
    was where we *wanted* to be,
        where it felt *right* for us to be.
They were times of touch.
We touched one another,
    and we were in touch with ourselves.
We touched the world around us,
    and we were in touch with that which underlies our world
        and upholds it.
Life on this earth holds promises one moment,
    and then *with*holds promises others.
And we experience how fleeting happiness can be.
How quickly the present moment moves on,
    leaving behind it only the past, *all* of the past.

There are times in our lives when we remember,
   and in the remembering there is a longing.
A wishing for what we had.
A searching for who we were.
A grasping for what we lost.
Longing is the price we pay for having loved.
Had we not known closeness,
   we would not mourn its absence.
Had we not known joy, we would not miss its passing.
Had we not known contentment,
   we would not know the sorrow of being without it.
It is one thing to say this, to think it.
It is altogether another to *feel* this, and to *live* it,
   hour after hour, feeling after feeling.
We cannot recreate the past.
It is beyond bringing back.
But—the past *was* once.
And that can *never* be taken from us.
Something of what we had is with us still.
And it always shall be.
Growth we experienced.
Understanding we gained.
Love we shared.
Memories we formed.
And memories that will in time form us.
There are times in our lives when we remember,
   and this is one of them.
A time when our remembering is more than remembering.
It is also anticipating.
It is allowing our remembering to also be a hope
   and a pledge, carried on these words:
In the summer sun and fields of brightness,
   we will remember.
In the autumn haze and blazes of color,
   we will remember.
In the winter chill and blankets of whiteness,
   we will remember.

And in the warmth of spring and bursts of new life,
   we will remember.
In the breezes that caress the leaves, as well as our own hair,
   we will remember.
In the winds that fan the hillsides, as well as our own hearts,
   we will remember.
In the waves that wash upon quiet shores,
   as well as our own hushed souls, we will remember.
With everything that is permanent, and with all that is passing,
With everything that is majestic, and with all that is common,
With everything that causes us sorrow,
   and with everything that carries us in joy,
     we will remember again and again and again.
As long as we have life, we will remember.
And in the remembering,
   that which we have had will be with us still.
That which we have experienced will inform us again.
That which we have shared will help us share in new ways.
That which we have loved will encourage us to love again,
   and to love even more freely, and even more fully.
There are times in our lives when we remember.
And in the remembering there is a promise.
There is a hope.
There is a conviction.
The conviction that what we have known was *real*.
It *is* real.
And it *shall* be real,
   as long as the sun shall set,
     and as long as it shall rise again.
So: let us remember.
And in the remembering, let us look forward.

© James E. Miller

This published transcript cannot be copied, distributed, or used for any public gatherings without the permission of the author.